ARMED AND DANGEROUS

BRITAIN'S MOST DARING HEISTS

WENSLEY CLARKSON

CARLTON
BOOKS

THIS IS A CARLTON BOOK

Published in 2016 by Carlton Books Limited
20 Mortimer Street
London W1T 3JW

First published in 2013 under the title *Armed Robbery*

10 9 8 7 6 5 4 3 2 1

Text and design © Carlton Books Limited 2013, 2016

A CIP catalogue record for this book is available from the
British Library.

ISBN 978 1 78097 825 3

Printed **DUDLEY** CPI Group (UK) Ltd, Croydon, CR0 4YY

ARMED
AND
DANGEROUS

Contents

About the Author   6

Introduction   9

Author's Note – The Art of Robbery   15

The Flying Squad – Britain's Ultimate Thief Takers   17

The Mother of All Robberies   25

Welcome to the Dirty Dozen – Britain's Greatest Heists   29

1 The Big One   31
2 Walkie-Talkies Tell No Lies   55
3 Taking the Mickey   69
4 Snow Over Shoreditch   87
5 Men on a Mission   103
6 What Goes Around, Comes Around   135
7 Pointing the Finger   151
8 Operation Magician   161
9 Weak Spot   185
10 Who Played the Tune?   197
11 Tiger Attack   209
12 High Stakes   233

Postscript   249
Glossary   264
The Final Word – Watch Yer Back   267
Index   269

ABOUT THE AUTHOR

Wensley Clarkson's books have been published across the world and sold more than one-and-a-half million copies. He's also written movie screenplays and worked on numerous TV documentaries in the UK, US and Spain. Clarkson is renowned for his close contacts in the underworld and his books reflect that inside knowledge.

This book is dedicated to ALL the victims of robbery. It in no way tries to glamorize this brutal crime, which so frequently depends on the fear of violence to succeed.

"All my life I wanted to be a bank robber. Carry a gun and wear a mask. Now that it's happened, I guess I'm just about the best bank robber they ever had. And I sure am happy."

John Dillinger

Introduction

It's certainly tempting to admire the perpetrators of many of the robberies you are about to read about. Take the £40 million so-called super-heist on London's Graff jewellery store in 2009 (see page 233); it was all captured on video by CCTV cameras and a bystander. The footage seemed more like a Hollywood movie than reality. Many even believed the Graff heist harked back to an earlier time, when audacity and sheer nerve alone were the key qualities necessary for those aspiring to acquire rapid criminal wealth.

Many old-timers in British criminal circles still look back through somewhat rose-tinted glasses at what is called the "golden age" of armed robbery – the 1970s and early '80s – when *blaggers*, as armed robbers were known, were king and well-drilled *firms* operated with what seemed like military precision.

Sometimes wearing disguises, or just plain boiler suits, they'd storm banks and hijack cash-in-transit wagons. Working mainly in and around London, they netted hundreds of thousands in used notes – and occasionally the odd million or three. But the stakes were high and the sentences handed down to those who were caught, often after being informed on by colleagues who'd turned "supergrass", were Draconian. Some even paid the ultimate "price" – amid rumours that the police had an unofficial shoot-to-kill policy when it came to stamping out armed robbery.

More sophisticated players emerged in the 1990s; ones who realized there was less risk and bigger cash returns to be had in top-end drug dealing – and in shrewd investment of the proceeds. Many former bank and money-van robbers – usually the more intelligent ones – got stuck into this new way of "grafting". It brought an end to the mask-and-shotgun era – and introduced the concept of large-scale, US-style organized crime to the UK for the first time.

Shady underworld activities, largely hidden from view and steeped in intrigue, are far less understandable to the man in the street who is struggling to pay the bills – and therefore far less acceptable. The armed robbers of yore were up front and in yer face. It may be cowardly, in one sense, to terrorize security guards and cash workers, but it also takes some courage to hit back at society in such a flagrant manner. A quick vault over the counter waving a gun and shouting, "Fill the bag!" may appeal to even the most law-abiding citizen in desperate financial straits (so long as nobody gets hurt). Few would consider carrying out such a crime, however. Not just because it is wrong, but also because they probably would not have the nerve, or *the bottle*, as it's known in such circles. Hence the inevitable vicarious satisfaction from the actions of some of the *Big Jobs* described here.

Despite the obvious terror such events inflict on the innocent, the fact is armed robbery still has the power to inspire admiration, however misplaced. The images of the sharp-suited Graff raiders walking purposefully into the shop make for compelling viewing. Like Johnny Depp's Dillinger strolling into the First National Bank in the 2009 Hollywood gangster epic *Public Enemies*, they walked past the guard, cool as you like, acting as if they owned the place.

Away from the camera, the plunder begins. With mesmerizing swiftness the Graff robbers scoop up the booty – a record haul including around 40 watches, rings, brooches and necklaces worth up to £1 million each – and they're gone in less than three minutes, leaving behind just a small cloud of gun smoke and a whiff of cordite.

Dillinger, as played by Johnny Depp, boasted that he could rob a bank in, "About a minute… 40 seconds… flat." A fully-fledged public hero, he was shot dead in a police ambush.

The trouble is that often the perpetrators of the most spectacular heists are unprepared for the scale of the booty they steal. Disposing of tens of millions of pounds in gold, cash or jewellery is a complicated business. As in most high-profile cases, many of those responsible for the robberies are soon captured and receive decades behind bars for their efforts. Odds on it will be the same for most blaggers. There is nothing to be admired about that.

Yet, after drugs, robbery remains Britain's most profitable crime. It's not an easy reality to handle, is it? Over the past 50 years, Britain has turned into a gold rush for the country's underworld. And when robbers spend their millions, they even help keep many legitimate businesses afloat, especially in our tough inner-city areas.

Today, ever-shrinking police recruitment combined with officers who have been assigned away from the usual criminal haunts has left the way clear for robbers to thrive once again. In addition, the spiralling cost of living has even pushed some formerly law-abiding citizens into a life of crime.

One senior policeman told me it is harder now than ever before to monitor the movements and activities of criminals in the UK. He said: "A lot of them come here from abroad using false names. We have no local knowledge anymore. People are flooding this country from places like Eastern Europe and we haven't a bloody clue who any of them really are."

Successive governments have promised to freeze the assets of crime bosses and to impose multi-million-pound fines on any companies helping known villains. But like so many politicians' promises, it has become a matter of easier said than done. To date, only a small percentage of criminals has had their ill-gotten gains confiscated successfully. The rest of them continue to thrive.

A succession of Home Secretaries has insisted that targeting businesses and individuals linked to these so-called "super-gangsters" will eventually smoke them out. But one former south London robber tells me from his £5 million villa on the Costa del Sol: "They're living in cloud cuckoo land. No one's gonna stop these characters making millions every year off crime."

A National Criminal Intelligence Service (NCIS) study into Britain's new crime wave revealed that hundreds of robbery gangs are actively working at any one time in the UK. Takings from such crimes are laundered through reinvestment in pubs, restaurants, clubs and even banking, this decade's version of an open-air used-car lot. Criminals also dip in and out of property deals, often working with "legit" nominees. One well-known London property dealer who owed £600,000 to a gangster was shot dead after failing to come up with the cash owed on a deal after he had been greedy (or stupid) enough to go into "partnership" with a well-known "face".

Now many within Britain's police forces are pushing to introduce New York-style so-called "zero tolerance" into the UK. Ironically, some notorious criminals have been driven over here from the US in recent years because of that very same policy.

But what of the future for Britain's underworld? Will all the old-school gangsters survive as numerous others – most of whom are foreign – continue to muscle in on Britain's criminal hinterlands?

HM Revenue and Customs and the NCIS have set up specialist squads to prioritize the monitoring and infiltration of organized-crime gangs operating in Britain. But it seems highly unlikely that these steps will prevent the continued emergence of numerous villains who have come here from all over the world. Some foreign gangsters even use local "faces" to front their operations in the UK. "That way, no one really knows what they're up to," explained one old-school British hood.

So, ironically, these sinister, often nameless, foreign gangsters are helping the lower-end British-born criminals survive. "No one dares cross these foreign gangs because most of them are much colder than us," bank robber and south London face Gordon McShane told me. "One wrong move and you're dead. It's as simple as that." As one senior Scotland Yard detective also told me: "The UK is full of rich pickings for foreign criminals, and it's going to take more than a few brave words from a couple of politicians to clean out the vermin."

So there we have it: hidden beneath this country's facade as one of the world's most civilized places is a "netherland" of criminality. Britain truly is a place where robbery still pays.

One, two! One, two! And through and through
The vorpal blade went snicker-snack!
He left it dead, and with its head
He went galumphing back.

JABBERWOCKY

A poem by Lewis Carroll (1832–98)

AUTHOR'S NOTE –
THE ART OF ROBBERY

Here's the archetypal, old-fashioned armed robber. He's born into desperate poverty and abused at the hands of some brutal adult or other. He learns the power of fear and of the fist at a tender age. Then he's in and out of criminal institutions from his mid-teens. Life was never easy for these sorts of characters. There were few options available to them, so they choose the path of an armed robber.

It's a profession dominated by the dynamics of fear, fast cars, faster money and spontaneous, yet controlled, violence. It's about balancing brute force with a razor-sharp mind and, most important of all, sheer bloody-minded instinct. Every escape route needs to be mapped out. Every bad egg has to be discarded before they land you in the shit. Because when you're leaving the scene of a crime at 100mph, just one forced error means you're dead.

This book features some of the most daring armed robberies in British criminal history. It reveals the secrets behind the headlines and explains why these crimes have gone down in the annals of underworld folklore. But this book is much more than just another true crime anthology. *Armed and Dangerous* highlights many of the fascinating characters behind these robberies, rather than just chronicling the crimes themselves. For that is where the key lies to what villains still call to this day, the so-called "Art of Robbery". These stories are told with intelligence and from an insider's perspective because I know many of the villains and have spent the past 25 years ducking and diving through the underworld as one of Britain's best-selling true-crime authors.

In *Armed and Dangerous*, while I've tried to chart the development of robbery in the UK over the past 50 years, it's also inevitable that I've missed out a few of the characters who have helped create the villainous fabric of our nation. So, to those individuals I say sorry, although I'm not sure if any of them will mind!

The intention of *Armed and Dangerous* is not only to chart the history of the UK's robbery epidemic but also to reveal for the first time the chilling activities of the latest, new breed of robbers who are once again turning our streets into the hold-up capital of the world.

Overall, this book's intention is to expose the past and present existence of an underbelly of robbers, where crime continues to thrive amid great wealth and civility. It's a unique combination you won't find anywhere else in the world, and I hope you enjoy reading this book as much as I have enjoyed writing it.

Wensley Clarkson, London, 2016

THE FLYING SQUAD: BRITAIN'S ULTIMATE *THIEF TAKERS*

In 1919, shortly after the end of the First World War, police Inspector Walter Hambrook led a team of Scotland Yard detectives given special dispensation to arrest criminals anywhere in the Metropolitan Police District. This unique squad maintained surveillance on the streets from a horse-drawn carriage van, which was actually a canvas-covered Great Western Railway van with spyholes cut in the side.

Criminals soon dubbed them "the heavy mob", and this handpicked squad of police officers investigated some of the Met's most high-profile cases, concentrating mainly on armed robberies. In the squad's early days, London was experiencing a crime wave with large numbers of men recently released from the armed forces emerging onto the streets of the capital, many of them hardened to violence after experiencing the carnage of the Western Front.

The squad struck fear into the underworld by nabbing known criminals, including robbers, housebreakers and pickpockets, off the streets. The heavy mob also went undercover in pubs and clubs, where informants provided information on other criminals. It was the first time the police had officially used criminals in such a way. As a small unit of Branch C1, Central CID, they were known as the "Mobile Patrol Experiment".

Those early units enjoyed rapid crime-busting success and in 1920 were provided with two motor tenders capable of a top speed of 35mph – the speed limit at the time was just 20mph. A *Daily Mail* journalist at the time referred to them as "a flying squad of picked detectives", and the name stuck. The Squad's nickname in rhyming slang is "The Sweeney" from Flying Squad / Sweeney Todd, the notorious Fleet Street barber who turned his customers into meat pies and is these days generally regarded as a cliché.

The Flying Squad's primary function to this day is to detect and prevent armed robbery. They even use specially trained drivers, recruited from the uniformed divisions of Scotland Yard and given the honorary title of Detective Constable while serving in the Squad. By 1929, The Sweeney had evolved into a superbly organized London police unit of 40 officers led by a C1 Branch Detective Superintendent.

However, by 1938, the nation's police forces were reckoned to be at least 10,000 men under strength. London was once again overrun by petty criminals, yet the Metropolitan Police had only 1,400 detectives out of a force of 20,000 men. Public attention focused on the more glamorous activities of those small, elite teams employed in the Special Branch and the Flying Squad. But only 400 of these men were actually based at Scotland Yard.

Back then, a police constable's pay started at 62 shillings

a week (about £5 in today's money), with six shillings rent allowance and one shilling boot allowance. Decent digs at the time cost around 30 shillings and the only alternative was the grim police section house. Bobbies on the beat were still regarded with outright hostility by the poor, and it was hardly surprising that many policemen were susceptible to bribery and made free use of "Johnny Wood" – their truncheon – when not getting a slice of any profit made from a crime.

Then in the 1950s came the fearsome antics of postwar criminal legends Billy Hill and Jack Spot, plus the birth of gangs like the Krays. This sparked yet another resurgence of the Flying Squad, led by characters such as notorious detective Tommy Butler, who considered himself virtually above the law when it came to nailing down the "bad guys".

Butler, an unmarried, 24-hours-a-day policeman, had little or no interest in anything other than police business. He often worked into the early hours in his office at Scotland Yard and lived on sandwiches and food from the police canteen. He looked like an emaciated concentration-camp survivor and in his twisted mind everyone was a potential criminal – it was only a matter of time before they were all behind bars.

Butler's respect for justice and fair play was non-existent. Other policeman feared him, not because he was an upstanding officer but because of his manic, single-mindedness. It was this fear that stopped Butler rising to a higher rank in the force, not to mention the rumoured "bungs" he'd received from some of the capital's most notorious villains. To head the notorious Flying Squad, Butler would have had to be made a chief superintendent, but he was not allowed to go any higher by his superiors.

These days, Butler's dubious methods would have been

easily exposed by standard forensic science. But, in the 1950s and '60s, re-written statements and the planting of "bent" evidence regularly helped convict many so-called criminals.

The hard-nosed image of the Flying Squad back then left detectives wide open to accusations of corruption in the form of detectives either turning a blind eye to what was going on in return for a cut of the action or – if the information led to the recovery of stolen property – pocketing some of the reward money that the detective claimed on the informant's behalf. A strategically placed officer could also, for a fee, ensure bail was granted, hold back evidence and details about past convictions from a court, or pass on to a person under investigation details of a case being made against him or warnings about police operations in which he could become compromised. Corrupt officers also held onto a proportion of whatever valuables they recovered during an inquiry.

And in the middle of this virtual war between cops and robbers, security van hold-ups and bank robberies began to get a lot harder to pull off. This resulted in blaggers becoming even more desperate and dangerous. By the late 1960s, security guards were being used to escort large quantities of cash, which meant the robbers had to step up the levels of threats and resort more frequently to violence if they were to continue robbing with abandon on the streets of Britain's big cities.

In 1971, the Flying Squad came under close public scrutiny when the *Sunday People* revealed that its head, Commander Kenneth Drury, had been on holiday in Cyprus at the home of infamous Soho pornographer Jimmy Humphreys – a man with nine convictions to his name, including a spell in Dartmoor prison. Drury was served with disciplinary papers and suspended. He immediately resigned rather than face a full disciplinary hearing. But before doing so he wrote an article for the *News of the World* claiming that Humphreys had been one of his informants.

The furious pornographer – aware of the effect that such a claim could have on his relationships with many of his underworld associates – responded a week later through the columns of the same newspaper. He claimed he'd never received any money from Drury and had in fact wined and dined the police chief on a total of 58 occasions, during which Humphreys always picked up the bill. Drury later said it was "absolutely essential" for Flying Squad officers to mix socially with people connected with the criminal fraternity.

The problem with Drury's philosophy was that it left detectives wide open to accusations of corruption. Criminals would happily help police in an effort to divert attention from their own activities while at the same time obtaining, through the usefulness of the information given, a degree of protection from prosecution. Some London *faces* were even collecting cash rewards for pointing the police in the right direction, which then enabled them to pursue all their illegal activities unhindered.

In the 1970s, jury nobbling and interference with star witnesses was virtually a weekly occurrence at London's big courts, including the Old Bailey. The Director of Public Prosecutions (DPP) regularly objected to bail applications by villains on the basis that there was a "strong fear" of interference with witnesses.

Not surprisingly, Scotland Yard tried to overhaul its Flying Squad completely following the Drury revelations. Officers formed a central robbery squad run from a co-ordinating unit at Scotland Yard with four smaller groups strategically placed around London. The message to blaggers was loud and clear: "We are out to get you."

Detective Chief Supintendent Albert Wickstead, aka "The Grey Fox", head of the Yard's Serious Crimes Squad, sanctioned the Flying Squad to carry out raid after raid in 1973, which resulted in 235 officers taking 93 men and one woman into custody. One senior detective even told the *Daily Express* at the time: "The other side have never been hit so hard."

But then so-called supergrasses became – in the1970s – the key to so-called police success. The Flying Squad began actively persuading members of close-knit gangs to inform on robberies in advance. Perhaps the most notorious of all supergrass cases was the controversial chit-to-freedom that bank robber Bertie Smalls negotiated from Britain's law-keepers. Smalls became one of the most hated men in the London underworld as a result of "joining the other side". Many villains said they'd "gladly kill that bastard for nothing. He's vermin and should be wiped off the face of this earth."

Meanwhile, the Flying Squad regularly hauled in up-and-coming villains, suspecting they were connected to particular crimes even though they had no way of actually proving it. Some professional robbers were even approached by crime bosses to help frame high-ranking police officers, just before the police were due to give evidence in major trials. The aim was to smear their names to such an extent that their evidence would be seriously questioned in court.

The Flying Squad became obsessed with catching robbers

preying on security vans, which meant the police spent much of their time chasing their tails. On payday – which by this time was now on Thursdays – many Flying Squad detectives were simply sent onto the streets of London to look out for robbers. The reality was that the police simply weren't prepared or equipped for the latest surge in robberies and it became a perfect time for young robbers to thrive.

However, the tables started to turn when the Flying Squad unofficially issued a chilling message to the robbers of London: "*You'll be shot dead if you carry arms.*" To some criminals at that time, the police had become judge and executioner all rolled into one. And all it really did was stiffen their resolve to beat the police by whatever means.

The Flying Squad, by this time newly located to Limehouse Police Station in the middle of the East End, were single-mindedly trying to rip London's robbery gangs apart. It would lead to cat-and-mouse games lasting for at least two decades that were peppered with accusations ranging from bribery to the alleged participation of certain officers in actual robberies.

But the successes of the Flying Squad in the 1980s and early '90s undoubtedly helped create a vacuum, which would eventually be filled by the immigrant gangsters who have flooded into the UK over the past 20 years.

As one recently retired Flying Squad officer told me: "It's a totally different ballgame these days. We don't even know who most of these new foreign robbers are so how can we hit 'em hard? It's mission impossible."

THE MOTHER OF ALL ROBBERIES

KLM Airline Offices, Holborn, Central London, 21 September 1954

It was the ultimate precursor to the UK's most famous heist of all time – and it helped cement postwar Godfather Billy Hill's reputation as the undisputed boss of the 1950s' London underworld. The blaggers got away with two boxes containing £45,500 in gold bullion when a company lorry was hijacked at the KLM offices during rush hour. Hill was the police's prime suspect, even though at the time of the robbery Hill was in the offices of notorious journalist Duncan Webb at the *Sunday People* telling his favourite reporter yet another version of his life story as "Boss of the Underworld"; his autobiography was due to be published in the following Sunday's edition.

Hill, 43, even encouraged Webb to publish details of the KLM raid because he was so proud of it. He wanted the world to know all about this "brilliant" criminal enterprise, without actually ever admitting he was behind it.

The sheer audacity of the KLM job left the great British public, not to mention the rest of the world, gasping. "It was a ground-breaking blagging. No doubt about it," says master criminal Freddie Foreman. "The KLM job told us all that we had to step up to the mark and begin running professional teams of robbers, because there were rich pickings out there if we got our acts together." Even small-town American papers ran stories about the London robbery on their front pages.

Multiple phone taps were authorized by the top brass at the Yard and Billy Hill and his associates enjoyed winding up the cops by laying non-stop false trails over the phone. To add to the confusion, the police were inundated with calls from the general public telling them where the gold was hidden. One caller got in touch with the Flying Squad and told them the gold was hidden in a house in Lavender Hill by a bloke called "Guinness". Of course, it was all a mickey take referring to the film *The Lavender Hill Mob*.

Eventually, the long arm of the law managed to locate the van used in the raid to nick the gold plus a couple of sets of false number plates, but nothing else. When the Flying Squad pulled in all of Hill's mob, they discovered every one of them had a stone-cold alibi: two of them were reporting a road accident in Southend when the robbery took place; another was in a club in the West End; and so it went on.

Inevitably the police then went after the man himself and on 27 September 1954, just six days after the heist had taken place, dozens of officers raided Hill's toy warehouse HQ and his suite of offices in the East End, both of which he'd owned for years. Hill just happened to be on his way to the toy premises early that morning when he noticed a plain-clothes policeman in the street near his warehouse. He immediately hailed a cab, drove past the building, where he spotted dozens of plain-clothes men hanging around outside, and went straight to his solicitor's office. He then made a statement denying any involvement in the KLM job before accompanying his solicitor back to his premises.

Following a search lasting nine hours and featuring dozens of policemen, not a single item linking Hill to the KLM job was ever found. The Yard made several similar raids all over London in the weeks that followed but failed to discover any trace of the gold. Some years later, Hill claimed that, within hours of the raid, the bars of gold had been smelted down with some copper and silver so that no expert in the world could positively identify the new metal as being connected in any way to the gold that had been stolen.

As Freddie Foreman says today: "That was the classiest job of all. Trouble is it made us all think we could do just as well, which served as a wake-up call to the cozzers as well."

Nine years later, in the spring of 1963, Billy Hill had a meeting in an upstairs room at his latest favourite pub, The Star in Belgravia, at which he proposed funding what was to become known as "The Great Train Robbery", using the proceeds from a number of robberies he'd secretly financed, including the KLM job. However, the gang's leader, Bruce Reynolds, turned down the offer because Hill wanted a 60 per cent share of the proceeds.

Hill later said that not reducing his 60 per cent demand was the biggest regret of his life. When a London tabloid reporter tracked him down to a casino in Cannes just after The Great Train Robbery was carried out, he said: "I know nothing about it. Ring up Scotland Yard yourself. Now, if you like. Book plane tickets back to London, if you care to do so. I am so flicking mad about all the publicity without the money to go with it."

WELCOME TO THE DIRTY DOZEN – BRITAIN'S GREATEST HEISTS

1. THE BIG ONE
(The Great Train Robbery)

"In the old days you had this thing, you don't do post offices, banks and trains because they're Establishment. Then in the sixties, people began to realize that anything was fair game. The Establishment had been caught out. People realized that politicians, people we looked up to, were just as bent and people lost respect. People began to realize it was all a big con."

Former blagger **Eric Mason**

Ledburn, Buckinghamshire, 7 August 1963, 1.30am

It was a warm summer's evening. As village clocks chimed 1.30am in the English countryside just 40 miles north of London, the three-ton lorry and two Land Rovers moved down moonlit B-roads watching the shrubs and hedgerows flashing past in their headlights. Radios were tuned into the police frequency, but there was no activity. The convoy eventually pulled up near Bridego Railway Bridge just after 2.00am, having deliberately taken a long route round. Everyone disembarked and huddled in groups by the side of the track while walkie-talkies were given one final check. Just before 2.30am, they walked up the track to a point known as Sears Crossing to go over the plan one last time.

Typically, one of the "team", Charlie Wilson, 31, even had time for a few quips with his old friend Gordon Goody, 33.

"Gordon'll buy a new motor, won't you Gordon?" he said.

"If I can afford it," replied Goody.

"You can afford a Bentley Continental now," Wilson grinned.

"I wish I could. I'm fuckin' skint at the moment," responded Goody, his caution with money already legendary.

Wilson looked at Goody for a beat or two and then – using the team's colour-coded nicknames – said: "For fuck's sake, Blue, put your mask on. You're so ugly."

Laughing, Goody pulled his stocking mask down over his face. By 3am they were in position. It was time to go to work.

Minutes later two gang members rigged the signal so that it would appear red at the isolated crossing just before the bridge. They didn't disturb the electronic "fail-safe" gadgets, but covered the green signal with a glove and shone flashlights through the red panel of the signal. The train – which was exactly on time – halted precisely where they wanted it to. So far so good.

As train driver Jack Mills, 58, and his engineer David Whitby, 26, stepped down to see what was wrong with the signals, they were seized by a group of the bandits, who were now wearing silk stockings and balaclavas over their heads. At the same time, another section of the robbery team uncoupled the first two coaches, while postal workers in the remaining seven cars continued their routine unaware of the drama unfolding at the front of the train.

That's when Buster Edwards, 31, bludgeoned train driver Jack Mills with a cosh after the train driver had dared to hesitate about taking the train down the track to Bridego Railway Bridge, where the gang's lorry was waiting. Wilson eventually stepped between Edwards and Mills and with his bright blue eyes gleaming told the driver, "Don't worry, mate. No one's gonna hurt you now." Only then did Mills agree to steer the train down the line.

After arriving at Bridego Bridge, one of the gang shouted, "Get the guns", to frighten the Post Office sorters. Another team member lifted up Wilson high enough so he could use his cosh to smash the window of the carriage. Once in, Wilson ran at the men piling sacks against the door with his cosh raised; they turned and ran past him down the coach to where another gang member whipped them across the shoulders and told them all to lie face down. One of the robbers then used an axe to smash the padlock to the door containing the mail sacks. Minutes later the gang were using a human chain to sweep 120 mail sacks containing cash and diamonds into their three-ton lorry.

Back up front, robber Bobby Welch, 34, was now attending to injured train driver Jack Mills and his colleague David

Whitby. Then Wilson re-appeared and gave them each a cigarette. Crouching down besides the terrified Mills, Wilson wiped the blood off his face with a rag. Gang leader Bruce Reynolds, 32, later recalled: "Wilson made him comfortable, patching him up and offering him a cigarette as they sat on the grass verge beside the tracks.

"I think you're a real gentleman," Mills told Wilson.

Wilson then asked: "Do you want any money? We'll leave it on the grass verge for you."

But Mills shook his head.

After precisely three minutes had been counted down by Reynolds on his stopwatch, he announced: "That's it, chaps."

Wilson then chipped in: "But there's only a few left."

"Sod 'em," said Reynolds. "Time's up, let's get on the road."

Moments later, the gang swept off in their two identical Land Rovers and lorry.

The entire operation had taken just 15 minutes.

As the robbers drove steadily through the grey pre-dawn Buckinghamshire countryside, Wilson fiddled with the radio to try and check on the police movements. Suddenly the voice of American crooner Tony Bennett singing "The Good Life" came over the airwaves. It was the perfect epitaph. The others began laughing and then they all slapped each other on the back for the umpteenth time that hour. As fellow robber Tommy Wisbey, 34, later recalled: "We'd got the big prize. It was a feeling of elation. I think it would have been harder taking sweets off a baby."

Back at Sears Crossing, one of the Post Office assistant inspectors and a colleague scrambled out of the smashed-up coach and headed back along the tracks, where the remainder of the train was stranded. On the way, they met a guard, told him what had happened and they all raised the alarm.

At 4.30am the train robbery team pulled up in front of their hideout, Leatherslade Farm, exactly on schedule. It was only 12 miles from the scene of their audacious crime. At that moment the gang's shortwave radio crackled into life: "You won't believe this," said one policeman over the airwaves, "but they've just stolen a train."

The mailbags were quickly unloaded and stacked along the living room walls and in the hallway of the farmhouse. Each bag was carefully checked for any homing devices. Then some of the group started ripping open the bags and began stacking bank notes in small piles. Soon, £1.2 million in five-pound notes and £1.3 million in one-pound and ten-shilling notes, making a total of around £2.5 million, were spread out inside Leatherslade Farm. There was a long pause as all of them looked at the extraordinary sight of the money literally piled high in front of their eyes. Then they jumped up and punched the air in delight.

Bruce Reynolds then wished fellow gang member Ronnie Biggs, 34, happy birthday and went to each man and shook their hands in thanks. Charlie Wilson laughed out loud as he pointed to a bag of money saying: "Look at that. There's eighty grand in that pile." Then a few of the gang started singing "I Like It", a recent hit record for Freddie and the Dreamers as they stared manically at the piles of cash. Some of the others even grabbed a handful of old pound notes and used them to light their cigarettes.

~ The amount stolen by the gang would be worth more than £30 million by today's standards. The average salary at the time was £20 a week and each gang member's share of between £100,000 and £150,000 was the equivalent of a huge win on the National Lottery. But before the big share-out could go ahead, a news flash on the radio sent ripples of panic through the gang.

"Cheddington, England – A well-drilled gang of about 30 masked bandits have ambushed a mail train and escaped with loot estimated at millions of pounds in perhaps the biggest robbery of all time. The job was executed at 3.15am, 40 miles north of London with precision and teamwork that pointed to the strategy of an underworld mastermind who has met with success in previous train and bullion robberies…"

The gang knew then that they'd probably have to go on the run because many of them had committed previous crimes, which were well known to the police. Robber Charlie Wilson even told fellow gang member Buster Edwards at the farm: "We'll have to go on our toes. Me, who's never been further than Southend."

The initial plan to lie low in the vicinity until the heat died down had to be abandoned, so it was decided to share out the money immediately. Everyone knew they had to go their separate ways quickly, but, naturally, they also wanted their *own* share in their *own* hands.

The gang members were all aware of how important it was to keep the money successfully – and separately – hidden from police. No traces of it would ever turn up at the homes of the various suspects. Each gang member firmly believed it was a matter of each man for himself. Many years later, Charlie Wilson was credited with being the "treasurer" after the robbery, and was said to be the only man who knew where the majority of the money was hidden and the precise size of each cut. Whatever the full extent of his power and influence over the others gang members may have been, Wilson revelled in his image as one of the robbery's main organizers. He wanted to prove that crime really did pay.

Besides the cash, there was also the question of how the farm would be "cleaned" of any clues that might give away the gang's identity if and when the police discovered their hideaway. Charlie Wilson even managed a light-hearted dig at his old friend Bruce Reynolds about his obsessive cleanliness as Reynolds fretted about making sure no clues were left behind that might help the police.

"Why don't you open a fuckin' office-cleaning business, you cunt," Wilson told him at the farm. "You'd be good at that."

Reynolds laughed and said: "Get on with it – you don't want to leave any dabs, do you?"

"Fuckin' dabs," Wilson said. "There won't be any fuckin' surface left in a minute, let alone fingerprints."

"That'll suit me fine, Chas," added Reynolds, as he looked at the line of men behind him, each with a damp cloth in his hand, wiping everything in sight.

Charlie Wilson was so hungry that morning at Leatherslade Farm he ate two salt beef sandwiches over which he poured a generous covering of salt from a Saxa container, unintentionally leaving a thumb print on it. All of the gang then changed into their "normal" clothing and set off individually for London at high speed in a variety of stolen vehicles, which they had driven to the farm earlier.

The gang's "robbery clothes" were left at the farm to be destroyed by two of the gang who had been carefully briefed to make sure no clues were left behind after the rest of the "team" had departed. They were then supposed to set fire to Leatherslade Farm after they had finished cleaning everything. But the "clean-up squad" left the before completing the job. The rest of the Great Train Robbery gang members never forgave them for failing in their duty.

The moment they saw the newspapers that same morning, the gang knew the police were going to move mountains to get them and that none of them was safe. Many of them believed the weak link in the chain was the gang's so-called legal representative Brian Field, 29, who was not a professional criminal and therefore prone to crack under police pressure.

Five days after the robbery, on Monday morning, Charlie Wilson rang Field at his office and asked him cryptically: "Has the dustman been?" It was a reference to the clean-up of Leatherslade Farm. Field assured him that everything had been taken care of, but Wilson still wasn't happy and started ringing around the rest of the gang to arrange a meeting. Eventually Wilson, Reynolds, Edwards and Roy James met at Clapham Common underground station. Wilson said he didn't trust the men who were supposed to have cleaned the farm after their departure. He wanted them to go back and do it themselves, but no one else agreed, so he didn't pursue the matter.

The following morning the gang held a second meeting, this time with "weak link" Brian Field, outside Holland Park underground station, in West London. Field was shaking with nerves and Charlie Wilson was so irritated with Field that the others had to restrain him from trying to hit the lawyer. Field assured the gang he hadn't let them down and even told them: "If I get pulled, I swear I'll never say anything. I'll never make a statement. I'll never put any of you in it, and all I ask in return is that you look after my wife."

The gang held another meeting later that same day. Reynolds later recalled in his autobiography: "We presented an incongruous quartet in that transport café – Buster and I immaculately suited and booted, Chas and Roy in smart casuals." Sitting around a bare wooden table, the group nursed steaming hot cups of tea and discussed the "farm problem". Eventually they agreed to go back to the farm that night and clear out all the mailbags, the only clue linking the property to the robbery. They were halfway through their second cup of tea when Buster Edwards popped out to get the afternoon newspaper. When he returned he slapped down the paper on the table without saying a word.

"HIDEOUT DISCOVERED" read the *London Evening News* headline. The article said that two Land Rovers bearing identical number plates and a lorry with an ingenious secret drawer in the middle of the floor, big enough to take a large suitcase had been discovered at the empty farm.

Gang members later said they felt the whole robbery was doomed from that moment onwards. "I'd always known we were gonna get nicked. Now, it was just a matter of time," Charlie Wilson told an old friend years later.

But back in that café, the gang tried to sound upbeat.

"Let's go down there any way – we can cop for whoever is there and clear out the place," said one of them, peering over his cup of tea. Bruce Reynolds later explained: "But it made no sense. There would be more Old Bill [police] down there than the passing-out parade at Hendon Police College."

The big question no one wanted to ask that afternoon was whether any of them were already police suspects. Certainly, Charlie Wilson had no idea that he'd left a thumbprint back at the farm on that salt container, although he and other gang members thought their criminal records meant a "pull" was inevitable in any case.

Just then, gang member Roy James, 28, interrupted all their trains of thought by jabbing at the newspaper. "Look at this! Fuckin' Tommy Butler's now in charge of the London end." Butler, born in Shepherd's Bush, had joined the Met in 1934. Four years later he'd become a detective and had climbed steadily through the ranks. He'd had three spells on the Flying Squad before becoming a Detective Chief Superintendent in July 1963.

None of the gang could come up with a quip to counter the shock they all felt about Tommy Butler's appointment. It later emerged that an informant in prison had told Butler that the gang behind the robbery were all from London, which had prompted his appointment as head of the investigation. This 50-year-old bachelor with receding hair, dark eyebrows and a thin, pointed nose like Mr Punch still lived with his mother and adored Western films, but he was a relentless pursuer of villains.

As the GTR team shook hands at the end of that meeting in the café, they knew it might be the last time they ever met together in the outside world.

Later that day, two of the gang members were in a car together on their way back to their South London homes when another report about the police discovery of Leatherslade Farm came on the radio. One of them turned to the other and said, "That's it then, we're nicked."

A few hours after the discovery of the farm, Scotland Yard's Detective Superintendent Gerald McArthur and Sergeant Jack Pritchard, his ex-Commando assistant, arrived at Leatherslade to assist Detective Superintendent Malcolm Fewtrell, head of Buckinghamshire CID. As Frank Cater, later to be Commander of the Flying Squad, put it: "With the Great Train Robbery, it seemed to us that the world of crime detection had changed overnight. A new elite of organized crime had grown up, syndicates of men, not necessarily with criminal records, who specialized in robbery. They considered themselves to be in business and, like any other successful businessmen, they insisted on their enterprises being properly supplied with advance finance – equipment and, in particular, information had to be bought."

Meanwhile, Fleet Street saw the robbery as a brilliant circulation winner. One of the first newspaper front-page headlines read: "£1,000,000 BIGGEST MAIL ROBBERY EVER" although that estimate proved to be way under what was really on the train. The headlines then developed into "WORLD'S BIGGEST TRAIN HIJACK", but still the true value of the haul was not revealed to the world.

It wasn't until a few days later that the *Daily Herald* front page read: "UP TO £2 MILLION" after embarrassed Postmaster General Reginald Bevins finally admitted how much was really on the train. When Buckinghamshire constabulary initially put up a £10,000 reward for information to help track down the robbers it seemed laughable.

One cartoon in the *Daily Express* days after the robbery caught the gang's eye and always made them laugh. It showed a dozen robbers sharing out the money with a caption: "…two million, four 'undred thousand, nine 'undred an' ninety-nine. That's British justice for yer, one short…" Another cartoon showed the head of Buckinghamshire CID, Chief Fewtrell in animated guise with a magnifying glass following a trail of bank notes left by a runaway robber with a sack on his back. It was a farcical image and showed how the robbers were already perceived to have humiliated the establishment in such dramatic fashion.

In prisons across the country, the Great Train Robbery was the talk of the landings because it epitomized every villain's dream of one day "getting lucky". The train robbery gang had already earned the respect of the entire underworld.

The cash had weighed one-and-three-quarter tons, yet it had disappeared without trace. How could it have been got rid of without attracting attention? The only numbers on the notes, which the banks were able to give the police, were on 15,000 £5 notes. The police were still embarrassed by the Eastcastle Street mail-van robbery of 1952 when £250,000 had vanished into thin air.

Tenacious workaholic Flying Squad chief Tommy Butler immediately ordered a careful re-examination of that robbery, plus two more of the best organized robberies in the history of British crime – a £250,000 bullion theft in Finsbury, in 1960; and the £62,000 payroll snatch at London Airport the previous year.

Meanwhile across the country there were numerous alleged "sightings" of the gang. In Warwickshire, police were trying to find a couple, aged between 20 and 30, who ran away from a hired car which had crashed into a garden wall at Berkswell, near Coventry. The couple offered £5 notes for a quick lift to Birmingham, 18 miles away. Further south, squads of detectives had raided two adjoining houses in Stavordale Road, Highbury, in north London. An Irishman in one of the houses said: "They were looking for fivers. They searched the house from top to bottom, but went away empty-handed."

Detectives at Prince's Pier, Greenock, in Scotland, screened 260 passengers bound for Montreal on the Cunard liner *Carinthia*. A steward said: "We have heard that two of the mail train gang are Canadians and may try to get aboard the *Carinthia*." Meanwhile, Lancashire County Police were desperately trying to trace the owner of a Ford Consul with the registration number 986 RO. The car, with two men in it, was seen in Newton-le-Willows, loaded with luggage. Did it contain some of the cash from the Great Train Robbery?

Over at Leatherslade Farm, Detective Superintendent Maurice Ray, 54, looking like a not particularly prosperous bank clerk, was directing the minute, inch-by-inch search of the property. He eventually found a number of fingerprints, which were sent to a police laboratory for analysis.

On 16 August, Fleet Street was claiming that police were hunting for a retired army officer who was the brains behind the robbery. The *News of the World* said the man was known as "The Major", but that his nickname should not be confused with a well-known, small-time London fence who used the same nickname. (It was later surmised this must have been a reference to Bruce Reynolds, whom many thought was an ex-British army officer known to some as "The Colonel".)

Another popular rumour was that one-time King of the London underworld Billy Hill had bankrolled the entire robbery from his retirement villa in the south of France. Hill told one reporter who knocked on his door in the Côte d'Azur: "Look, I know nothing about it. Ring up Scotland Yard yourself. Now, if you like. Book plane tickets for both of us back to London, if you care to do so. I am so flicking mad about all this publicity without the money to go with it." Behind Hill's irritation was a tinge of jealousy. As he later admitted to another criminal: "What a masterpiece of a job. If only I could have laid on something like that. Brilliant!"

So the train robbers had already written their place in the history books. The Great Train Robbery as it was now known across the world would dominate newspapers and TV news bulletins for many months to come as the police – under the command of the dogged Butler – began to unravel the crime.

Later that same day – 16 August – two motorcyclists spotted a couple of suitcases in woodland in the Surrey hills, near Dorking, just south of London. The cases contained more than £140,000 in cash from the robbery. A hotel bill made out in the name of Brian Field, the solicitor the gang feared was their "weakest link", was found in one leather case. Hours later, an inch-by-inch examination of a caravan site in Box Hill, Surrey, uncovered £30,000 hidden in the wall lining of a trailer owned by one of the robbers, Tommy Wisbey.

Then the results of fingerprint tests taken at Leatherslade Farm came back from the Scotland Yard lab. They showed that convicted robber Charles Frederick Wilson had handled the Saxo salt container at the farm and that two other known criminals, Bruce Reynolds and Jimmy White, had been there as well. Tommy Butler was delighted, although some Scotland Yard officers were already muttering that milk-drinking Butler was trying to turn the GTR investigation into a one-man show. His bosses didn't care just as long as he got results.

At 1.15pm on 22 August 1963, just 14 days after the so-called crime of the century had been committed, Scotland Yard issued descriptions of the three man wanted in connection with the Great Train Robbery, with Charlie Wilson top of their list. His photo was splashed across every newspaper in the land. A typical headline in the *London Evening Standard* read: YARD SEEK THREE MEN. By now newspapers no longer even had to refer to the train robbery in the headline. It was already *that* famous.

Less than two hours after that story first appeared, four Flying Squad cars turned up at Wilson's home in Crescent Lane, Clapham, while he was having lunch with his family. As Wilson was taken away in handcuffs, Pat and his three daughters watched from the front window. A search for the other two named men, Bruce Reynolds and Jimmy White, continued.

Wilson arrived at Cannon Row police station in a Ford Zephyr squad car just before 3.30pm on 22 August to be greeted by Tommy Butler. Butler told Wilson they were making inquiries into the train robbery and Wilson chipped in: "You obviously know a lot. I have made a ricket (balls up) somewhere, but I will have to take my chances."

Wilson, like all good professional criminals, denied all knowledge of the robbery and came up with a stream of alibis for where he was on the night of the crime.

Racing driver Roy James, known as "The Weasel", heard about Wilson's arrest on a car radio as he was driving back from motor-racing practice at Goodwood, Sussex. James turned to one of his mechanics and said: "They've nicked Wilson. The cops'll connect me to him now."

Then he stopped the car and bought a newspaper, which had photos of the three GTR suspects splashed across its front page. When James phoned his mother, she told him the police had already been to see her.

Tommy Butler and his train robbery team soon rounded up four more members of the gang with remarkable speed and tenacity. They were Roger Cordrey, 42, Ronnie Biggs, Jimmy Hussey, 34, and Tommy Wisbey and detectives had a call out for five other alleged robbers – Bruce Reynolds, John Daly, 32, Buster Edwards, Roy James and Jimmy White. Four others were also on Butler's chief suspects' list.

The robbers all refused to admit to anything as they might yet be found not guilty at their eventual trial. So when Ronnie Biggs was told by a prison officer inside Bedford Prison, "We've got one of your mates in here,

Charlie Wilson," Biggs responded: "Charlie Who? Never heard of him."

On 3 December 1963, Wilson tried to "negotiate" his way out of prison by offering one senior detective a £50,000 bribe to "lose" the evidence police had against him. Wilson claimed he was framed for the Great Train Robbery by corrupt cops who'd taken his fingerprint samples and ensured they were then conveniently "found" on that drum of Saxo salt. So he believed that offering another officer a bribe was nothing particularly out of the ordinary. Fifty thousand pounds in cash was left in a telephone box in Great Dover Street, just south of the Thames, in Southwark, but the policeman who had been offered the bribe had already told his superiors as soon as Wilson made the offer. And the £50,000 of missing train robbery money consisted of notes which were so mouldy that most of them were stuck together.

The gang's most feasible chance of freedom lay with their defence team at their coming trial. They each hired top lawyers with fine reputations among professional criminals.

Before the actual trial got underway – in early January 1964 – the wife of Brian Field claimed to police that an unnamed man had suggested to her that six of the jurors should be paid £500 each in order to influence the verdict at the trial. These sorts of incidents did nothing to help the robbers' cause as it made them look even more criminally inclined. Naturally, they all insisted that such attempts at jury nobbling were nothing to do with them.

The Great Train Robbery trial began at the Old Bailey on 20 January 1964, and the jury was locked away each evening at a secret location to prevent any more attempts at so-called jury nobbling. Prosecuting barrister Howard Sabin summed up the Establishment's view of the train robbery when he told the court that the raid was "a crime that strikes at the root of civilized society". The moment the gang members heard that phrase – they'd all pleaded not guilty – they rolled their eyes, because they knew that phrase meant none of them stood a chance.

When injured train driver Jack Mills delivered his testimony to a hushed courtroom in a quiet, shaky voice, Charlie Wilson whispered to Bobby Welch that he reckoned Mills was " a right fuckin' actor". The gang knew it looked bad for them. For the following two months they sat in the dock without muttering a word, resigned to being found guilty and thinking constantly about their next moves.

At 10.32am on Thursday, 27 March 1964, the all-male jury returned to give their verdict after being out for a record 66 hours and 56 minutes. The voice of the foreman shattered the silence in the Old Bailey court with one word: "Guilty." Over the next ten minutes he repeated it 18 times as the twelve gang members were dealt with. The tension mounted as, in turn, the prisoners, a warder at each of their sides, stood up to hear their verdict. They left the dock at the rate of one a minute.

The judge told them: "You have been convicted of conspiracy to rob a mail train and of armed robbery. The consequence of this outrageous crime is that the vast booty of something like £2.5 million still remains almost entirely un-recovered. It would be an affront to the public if any one of you should be at liberty in anything like the near future to enjoy those ill-gotten gains."

One young rookie police officer called Ken Rogers never forgot travelling with chief investigator Tommy Butler to the train robbers' trial on a number of occasions. Butler even insisted that Rogers be present on the day of conviction. As the robbers were being taken away, Butler turned to Rogers and said: "You are the youngest officer on the Flying Squad, take a good look at them as they will be over the wall soon."

Two days before sentencing, some newspapers alleged that the gang had offered to tell police where all the train robbery money was in exchange for reduced sentences. They could not have been further from the truth. As one friend of the gang said many years later: "No one would give the police the time of day, let alone the key to all that cash. In any case, they all had big plans for the future."

On Wednesday, 15 April 1964, ten members of the Great Train Robbery gang were brought to the Old Buckinghamshire Assizes Court to be sentenced. It was a sombre building with dark panelling and an enormous Royal coat of arms above the judge's throne. Mr Justice Edmund Davies, wearing the wig and robes of the Establishment, was flanked by the Sheriff of the County, also dressed in ceremonial attire. The barristers were wearing robes and wigs and the policemen were in their uniforms; of the principal players, only Wilson and the other gang members were wearing contemporary clothing. One of them later told a friend: "That summed it up, really. Them against us."

Before sentencing, Judge Davies told the gang members: "Let us clear out of the way any romantic notions of daredevilry. This is nothing more than a sordid crime of violence inspired by vast greed. All who have seen that nerve-shattered engine driver can have no doubt of the terrifying effect on the law-abiding citizens of a concerted assault of armed robbers. To deal with this case leniently would be a positively evil thing. Potential criminals who might be dazzled by the enormity of the prize must be taught that the punishment they risk will be proportionately greater."

Mr Justice Davies continued to the court: "It would be an afront to the public if anyone of you should be at liberty in anything like the near future to enjoy those ill-gotten gains. My duty is clear. If you or any of the other accused still to be dealt with had assisted justice that would have been strongly in your favour."

The train robber's sentences were the longest ever handed out to such a group of criminals in British history:

Ronald Arthur Biggs	Conspiracy to rob mail	25 years
	Armed robbery	30 years
Douglas Gordon Goody	Conspiracy to rob mail	25 years
	Armed robbery	30 years
James Hussey	Conspiracy to rob mail	25 years
	Armed robbery	30 years
Roy John James	Conspiracy to rob mail	25 years
	Armed robbery	30 years
Robert Welch	Conspiracy to rob mail	25 years
	Armed robbery	30 years
Charles Frederick Wilson	Conspiracy to rob mail	25 years
	Armed robbery	30 years
Thomas William Wisbey	Conspiracy to rob mail	25 years

	Armed robbery	30 years
Brian Arthur Field	Conspiracy to rob mail	25 years
	Conspiracy to obstruct course of justice	5 years
Leonard Dennis Field	Conspiracy to rob train	25 years
	Conspiracy to obstruct course of justice	5 years
William Boal	Conspiracy to rob mail	21 years
	Armed robbery	24 years (reduced to 14 years on appeal)
Roger John Cordrey	Conspiracy to rob mail	20 years
	Receiving stolen money	20 years (reduced to 14 years on appeal)
John Denby Wheater	Conspiracy to obstruct the course of justice	3 years

The gang was sentenced to a total of 573 years, but as the sentences were all to run concurrently, they were actually to serve sentences that amounted to 307 years, taking parole into account.

All the train robbers were put on a very special "Order 44", which meant heavy restrictions were placed on their movements inside prison. It was all part of a specific Home Office policy to separate the gang in order to ensure they didn't team up together to organize escapes. The gang saw it as yet more evidence that the Establishment were further punishing them.

One headline and story following the gang's sentencing summed up the mood of the nation: *THE GOLDEN FLEECE – They played for high stakes – a cool £2,600,031. And the Great Train Robbers earned the nation's grudging applause. But they lost. Now they must face the censure of the nation's laws.*

Flying Squad chief Tommy Butler admitted privately that he felt great sympathy for the families of the train robbers, who were going to have to manage on their own for a very long period of time. Butler was one of the old school, prepared to meet underworld informants at any time of the day or night. And it was Butler – the thin shouldered, uninteresting bank manager look-alike – who was always there at the final arrest.

AFTERMATH

While much has been written about Great Train Robber Ronnie "Our Man in Rio" Biggs, he was, in the words of one other train robber, "a complete fuckin' nobody" compared to Charlie Wilson, who was undoubtedly the most powerful villain to emerge from the team behind the so-called "Crime of the Century".

For after going on the lam following those outrageously long sentences for the GTR and then finally serving his time after being recaptured, Wilson morphed into a notorious bigtime drug baron. He might have made his name by committing the Great Train Robbery, but it was during his reign as a cocaine king that Wilson's reputation as an all-powerful character capable of cold-blooded brutality on the one hand and immense kindness on the other confirmed his status as one of the king's of the British underworld during the final quarter of the last century.

Overall, there is no doubting Wilson's life was a roller-coaster ride through five decades of crime, including a long spell in the Spanish sunshine and forays into the deadliest killing fields of all: South America. A meticulous organizer, Wilson was at the centre of a bizarre, sordid, crime-filled world – one that took him from the mean streets of south London to even harsher prison corridors, and from a quiet life on the run in small-town Canada to the heated, manic, cocaine-fuelled Costa del Sol.

And Wilson's obsession with greed and corruption eventually saw him descend into a living hell when his rivals decided to wipe him off the face of the earth – with the tacit approval of Spanish, British and US drug enforcement agencies.

But like so much connected to the GTR, Wilson's life and death provides a glance inside the real history of organized crime in Britain, starting with 1950s London crime bosses Billy Hill and Jack Spot followed by the Krays and then ending in Wilson's own brutal death in 1990.

Many other criminals feared Wilson and his love of pretty women had almost cost him his life on numerous previous occasions. But when he finally decided to "retire", he discovered the inevitable: that gangsters never rest in peace. A man on a bicycle arrived at Wilson's home near Marbella one sunny afternoon, pulled out a gun and shot him dead...

2. WALKIE-TALKIES TELL NO LIES

"Let Sherlock Holmes solve this one."

Daubed on wall of bank vault after robbery

Baker Street, London, 11 September 1971

The Great Train Robbers had opened up a huge wound in the Establishment, thanks to their highly publicized heist but, by September 1971, the Cynical Seventies had replaced the Swinging Sixties. And in the London underworld, a new breed of clinical, well-organized robbers who didn't hesitate to strike fear and trepidation into many victims was emerging. They didn't bother with any of the highly publicized antics enjoyed by the big-time villains of the previous decade. No, these characters were low-key professionals who thrived on keeping *out* of the limelight. They also happened to have a lot of London coppers in their pockets, just in case they were in need of any "help".

So, with Britain's boom days of the 1960s just a distant dream, new Conservative Prime Minister Edward Heath was struggling with the country's finances and the UK veered from one crisis to the next with alarming regularity. Striking miners and many others were being accused of crippling the nation.

When Heath swanned off to participate in the British victory in the Admiral's Cup yacht race, it outraged many working folk, who believed he should have remained glued to his desk at Number Ten throughout that long, hot uncomfortable summer as unemployment threatened to top the one million mark for the first time.

When, in early September 1971, Heath's Education Secretary Margaret Thatcher ended free school milk for children aged over seven years – and became one of the Britain's most unpopular politicians as a result – no one could have imagined that she'd overthrow Heath within a few years and go on to become one of the country's longest-serving premiers.

By the second week in September, the Troubles in Northern Ireland had escalated at an alarming rate following the death of 14-year-old Annette McGavigan, who was fatally wounded by a gunshot in crossfire between British soldiers and the IRA.

And then, in the middle of all this domestic turmoil, showjumper Harvey Smith was stripped of his winner's trophy when he outraged the upper classes by making a V-sign at the crowd at the British Show Jumping Derby.

However, in south London, a team of traditional, tightly-knit blaggers had their minds set on one lucrative target as they planned what they believed could turn out to be the heist of the century. They'd earmarked the second weekend in September as the perfect time to hit Lloyd's bank in London's Baker Street, famed as the fictional home to Conan Doyle's *master-sleuth* Sherlock Holmes.

Ironically, a number of the gang had become ardent readers of Holmes's books during earlier spells in prison. They found it highly amusing that their "target" was a bank neighbouring Holmes's apartment at 221b Baker Street – and had even decided to taunt the cops about this connection if they ever got the chance. No one knows to this day if any members of the gang realized how closely Conan Doyle's Sherlock Holmes short story *The Red-Headed League* resembled the crime they were about to commit, though. In it, Holmes and Dr Watson hide themselves in a bank vault in order to unmask a criminal mastermind.

By 11 September, with all the gang's preparations in place, it was time to go to work. Diana Ross might have been top of the single's charts with her pop classic "I'm Still Waiting", but the blaggers had decided they were not going to sit around a moment longer. They had no idea that an amateur radio ham called Robert Rowlands, from nearby Wimpole Street, would "tune into" their robbery for a live commentary and would ultimately help bring about their downfall.

Rowlands, 35, was one of tens of thousands of British amateur radio hams, who twiddled buttons and put on headphones every night to listen to the world at large. Rowlands ran his own financial company and lived in a fourth-floor flat in Wimpole Street, less than half a mile away from Baker Street. Getting into bed at 11.15pm on that Saturday night with a cup of tea and an Ian Fleming novel, he switched on his radio.

Rowlands tried to contact a fellow radio ham in Australia, but every time he touched the very sensitive dial he kept hearing other voices coming through much louder and clearer between the whistling noises and crackling. Initially he took no notice of what was being said, as his main priority was to bypass the "interference" and get a clear contact with his friend in Australia. But much to Rowlands's irritation, the voices continued to dominate the airwaves. He soon realized they were coming through on a wavelength only used by walkie-talkies, which meant they were undoubtedly coming from a source within a one-to two-mile radius of his own home. Rowlands had experienced "technical" problems like this before and had always found it highly annoying, but he believed there were ways around it, even though it would be time consuming and would prevent him from talking uninterrupted to his Aussie friend.

Rowlands was twiddling frantically with the dials on his cumbersome radio transmitter when he suddenly heard a man's voice talking in a flat, yet aggressive tone. There was something about the voice that told Rowlands he was listening to an illicit conversation. The voice was ordering someone on the other end of the line to switch off all equipment and stop hammering, as the "Old Bill" (criminal slang for police) had just pulled up outside and were very close by. Rowlands stopped dead in his tracks and listened avidly. Then he wondered if he was the victim of a huge practical joke.

Moments later, Rowlands heard the same voice in even more hushed tones. This time, however, the voice was swearing and in the middle of these expletive-laced references was mention of digging, as well as the rooftop where the other man on the line seemed to be located. Rowlands found himself more than just a little intrigued. He believed he must have stumbled upon some kind of criminal activity. Was he listening to a live commentary of a robbery?

Rowlands's suspicions were quickly confirmed when the conversation between the two men on the radio started up again. The main speaker said the police had now left the location. Then, suddenly, another voice came on the line. This one had a much stronger, harder south London accent.

The voice declared they now had about 400,000, and would let the other man know when they were coming out. The man then asked his associate if he was being heard "okay", to which his accomplice replied that he could hear him loud and clear, and wanted to know how much longer they would be in there.

Rowlands now realized for certain that not only had he stumbled on a robbery, but that it was also taking place very near to where he lived; although he still didn't appreciate just how big a robbery it was. He later recalled that when he'd heard the reference to "400,000", he decided it was probably referring to the theft of 400,000 cigarettes from a tobacconist's shop.

Rowlands then phoned the police and reported his suspicions to them, but, much to his frustration, the officer on the other end of the line failed to take his call seriously.

The policemen assumed Rowlands was just "another of those crazy radio hams" and said sarcastically that if he "heard any more funny voices" he should record them and let him know in due course. Outraged by the officer's attitude, Rowlands slammed down the phone and decided he'd do some more detective work himself, otherwise no one would take him seriously. So, using a cassette tape machine he was using to teach himself Spanish, he began recording the voices that were coming through on his radio transmitter.

Rowlands sat there for at least another half hour recording every word the "robbers" spoke. He soon concluded that this was a lot bigger than just the robbery of a tobacconist's shop. Now, armed with actual proof, Rowlands was determined to find another more responsive police officer, one who would have no choice but to believe his story. However, just before he was about to pick up the phone and call the police again, the conversations on the walkie-talkie became even more incriminating.

It was just after midnight and the man – who Rowlands now knew was on the roof of a building that was being robbed – was in the middle of a virtual running commentary when another new voice came onto the airwaves. This character identified himself as "Steve" and nervously told the rooftop lookout to switch off his walkie-talkie and stay on the roof of the "bank" all night. For the first time Rowlands now knew the specific nature of the robbers' target.

Just then the lookout said he was very worried about the plan for him to remain in place while the gang left for the night. But "Steve" told him: "Look, the place is filled with fumes and if security come in and smell them we are all going to take stoppo [make a hasty getaway] and none of us have got nothing, whereas this way we've all got 300 grand to cut up."

Another gang member then chipped in on the radio waves, telling the lookout: "You can't go now, we're almost there." The unequivocal response from the lookout was: "Money may be your god, but it's not mine, and I'm fucking off."

Radio ham Rowlands then heard a series of heated exchanges between the lookout and various members of the gang, including one voice that was definitely that of a woman. After a few more minutes and a further intervention by the female member of the gang, the lookout finally relented and agreed to remain on the rooftop overnight before signing off. "Steve" ordered the roof man to come back on the air with both radios at six o'clock the following morning.

While listening to all of this, Rowlands made at least three unsuccessful attempts to call the police again, but they weren't picking up. Eventually, he got through to his local police station and a constable arrived on Rowlands's doorstep ten minutes later. However, the constable then got called away almost immediately before he could listen to the walkie-talkie conversations that Rowlands had so carefully recorded.

By this stage Rowlands was at the end of his tether. Why was it proving so hard to tell the police that a bank robbery was being committed in their vicinity? It was frustrating beyond belief. Then, in despair and still in his dressing gown and slippers, Rowlands, as a last desperate measure, contacted Scotland Yard directly. Relieved to have got through to a detective who at least had the decency to listen to him, Rowlands was told by the officer that "the uniform branch don't know what they were doing" and the detective promised to send two Scotland Yard officers over immediately.

By now the radio exchanges had gone silent in keeping with the orders made by robber "Steve". Rowlands gathered together his tapes of the conversations and waited for the officers to arrive. Eventually, two detectives turned up, sat down with Rowlands and began listening to the tapes that he'd recorded.

"They sat on chairs by my bed and we stayed up all night," Rowlands later recalled. At dawn, another pair of plain-clothes officers joined them as they listened to every moment Rowlands had recorded.

Then, at 9am, the gang member called "Steve" came on air, telling the lookout: "We're going to finish off in here [the bank] and we shall be coming out early this afternoon and you'll just have to bluff, bluff your way straight down off the roof."

Then "Steve" used the word "bank" for the first time and the officers now had absolutely no doubt they were listening to a robbery in progress.

For the first time in nearly ten hours of listening, Rowlands's claims were finally being taken seriously. The police immediately called in radio detector vans in an attempt to trace the transmissions, but unfortunately, by the time Post Office engineers could be brought in to work from weekend leave, the walkie-talkie conversations had stopped altogether.

So Scotland Yard were left with no choice but to

begin checking on 750 banks in the inner London area, paying special attention to the 150 banks within a mile of Rowlands's home in Wimpole Street. It wasn't until Sunday afternoon, that two officers finally visited the Lloyd's Bank on the corner of Baker Street and Marylebone Road.

The officers saw nothing suspicious on the outside of the bank, which wasn't surprising since the blaggers had tunneled their way inside the premises from a nearby shop. The two PCs radioed back to the Yard to say they had found no signs of a forced entry; the 15-inch thick doors of the vault were intact and secured by a time lock. What they did not know at this point was that the raiders were just over 12 inches away from them, still inside the vault.

The police didn't discover them and within a few hours the team of blaggers had disappeared into the London underworld. An indignant Rowlands, later recalled: "They'd had ten hours to locate the raid while it was happening, yet didn't take any action until it was too late."

It wasn't until 9am on Monday morning when the bank opened for business after the weekend that the robbery was uncovered. Scores of empty safety deposit boxes were found broken open and lying all over the floor of the vault, their contents looted. The police quickly, albeit reluctantly, admitted that the robbery had just been pulled off within breathing distance, literally, of them. It was extremely embarrassing for Scotland Yard.

In the days following the raid, detectives gradually began to unravel the background to the job and even the police had to admit that the robbers had planned the heist with military precision and extreme professionalism. Initially, the blaggers had rented a leather goods shop called Le Sac, located just two doors down from Lloyds Bank.

The gang then tunneled a distance of approximately 50 feet under a fried chicken restaurant. They'd deliberately decided to dig over the weekend to avoid anyone hearing the noise of their equipment.

Then, using a thermal lance, they tried to "burn" through the 3ft of reinforced concrete that formed the floor of the vault. The floor was not wired to the alarm system, as it was thought to be impenetrable. However, the high-tech thermal lance didn't create a big enough hole, so the gang ultimately had to use explosives to get through instead.

Eight tons of rubble was excavated and left behind in the shop when the gang escaped with their haul, the contents of 268 deposit boxes estimated at the time to be worth in the region of £500,000. It has since been alleged that the haul was in fact worth in excess of £3 million, which, in 1971, made it the largest-ever bank robbery on British soil.

From evidence found at the scene, it seemed that the gang had made their escape around Sunday lunchtime, even though bank security chiefs insisted all the alarm systems had been working.

The story dominated the newspapers and TV for the next few weeks. One tabloid headline screamed "The Moles of Baker Street", while another exclaimed "Sewer Rats". The gang, just like the Great Train Robbery team from eight years earlier, had captured the public's imagination.

Rowlands's tape recordings and his radio were confiscated by embarrassed police officers and were not given back to him for six years. Rowlands later claimed that the police had told the editor of one newspaper that a top security D-Notice had been put on the story, banning publication, due to the "sensitive nature" of some of the contents of the safety deposit boxes.

At the time Rowlands believed it was to hide the police's extraordinary incompetence. Outrageously, the police even allegedly threatened to prosecute Rowlands for listening to an unlicensed radio station. That blow was eventually softened by a £2,500 reward from Lloyd's Bank.

The police were undoubtedly deeply embarrassed by the Baker Street robbery because they knew only too well that radio ham Rowlands's early phone calls to alert them to the crime might have helped prevent the actual robbery from being successful.

Eventually, Scotland Yard was forced to admit publicly that Rowlands had first rung them to report his suspicions more than 12 hours before the robbers had left the bank. The police tried to talk their way out of the embarrassment by pointing out that at no point had the robbers given away the location of the bank in any of their radio chats.

The police also insisted that when they finally visited the Lloyd's Bank in Baker Street, they could not get into the vault because the door was on a timer and that it did not look as though it had been broken into. As a result, the officers who called at the bank left the premises believing no robbery was taking place.

In the months following the robbery, a number of outrageous allegations began to surface, not just about the identity of the gang of bank robbers, or incompetent police officers, but about a member of the Royal Family.

It was alleged that a well-known Trinidadian activist and gangster called Michael X, who was operating in London at the time, had in his possession "certain compromising photos" of the Queen's sister Princess Margaret.

Stories about Princess Margaret's "colourful" love life had long been bandied about. She was rumoured to have had affairs with lovers, including Peter Sellers and a string of other well-known and some not so well-known faces about town.

One such character was the late tough-guy actor and gangster John Bindon, the boyfriend of a baronet's daughter, the actress and model Vicki Hodge. West Londoner Bindon visited the Caribbean island of Mustique (one of Princess Margaret's favourite hangouts) on a number of occasions, and did indeed meet and attend parties where the princess was present. It is alleged that she thought he was very amusing and that he often impressed her with his party trick of balancing five half-pint beer mugs on his manhood. (*My biography of Bindon concluded that the Princess and the gangsters conducted a six-month affair, which had the authorities so concerned that MI5 was brought in to keep it under wraps.*)

With such rumours travelling at breakneck speed on the grapevine, it was then alleged that the robbery had been masterminded by Britain's domestic security service, MI5, who offered the "job" to a gang of well-known villains. They were told they could keep all the valuables and money as long as they turned over the compromising photos of Princess Margaret to the authorities, who could then use them to neutralize Michael X's threat. Shortly after the bank raid, Michael X was tried in his native Trinidad for the murder of Joseph Skerritt, a member of his Black Liberation Army. He was found guilty and was hanged in 1975.

However, the real story behind the "walkie-talkie robbery", as it became known, will probably never come to light. Most of the loot was never recovered, but police did admit many years later that when the gang departed the scene of the crime they left a message for police. Spray-painted on the inside of the vault were the words: *Let Sherlock Holmes try to solve this.*

Scotland Yard's Flying Squad did eventually track down most of the robbers. Two years after the blagging, four men were tried for the robbery at the Old Bailey. They were Anthony Gavin, 38, a photographer from Dalston; Thomas Stephens, 35, a car dealer from Islington; and Reginald Tucker, 37, a company director from Hackney, who all pleaded guilty and each received 12 years' imprisonment. The fourth man, Benjamin Wolfe, 66, a fancy goods dealer from East Dulwich, pleaded not guilty, but was subsequently convicted and received eight years. He was the man who signed the lease on the shop used by the robbers. Two other men were accused of handling banknotes from the robbery, but they were never prosecuted. According to one press report, it was believed that the mastermind of the crime was another London car dealer, who was never apprehended.

AFTERMATH

The alleged story of the bank robbery and its so-called connection to the Royal Family 'scandal' was made into a movie called *The Bank Job*, featuring Hollywood star Jason Statham. It was claimed to be based on "certain real-life events", but this author believes it was largely a work of fiction.

3. TAKING THE MICKEY

"There was just thousands upon thousands of notes stacked up in neat little piles on the bare floor. The money was everywhere, inches deep on the floor."

Chainsaw gang member **Bernie Khan**

Banstead, Surrey, July 1978

In the 1970s, a team of robbers known as the "Chainsaw Gang" earned their place in criminal history by carrying out some of the most audacious blaggings ever seen in Britain. They specialized in highly dramatic hijackings of security vans and by July 1978 had struck so much fear into London's security guards that companies found it increasingly hard to recruit staff who were prepared to risk their lives on the roads of London and south-east England.

The gang was so well organized they even had a small army of underworld "tipsters" who told them about lucrative potential targets. That was how 38-year-old gang leader

Chopper Knight heard that each week a Security Express van picked up at least £250,000 in cash from a bank in the leafy town of Banstead, Surrey, on the outskirts of London and then headed back to the capital via a main road called Sutton Lane. This was just the type of big-money job Knight and his fellow gang members were after, especially since they specialized in using huge, fearsome chainsaws to cut open armoured vans "like butter".

Within weeks gang member Jimmy Moody, 36, was sitting in his Ford Granada watching the home of the Banstead Security Express van's driver. Moody noted down all relevant times and locations. He even followed the man to work and saw him pick up a colleague en route. He then watched as the man started his day at the wheel of the security van, collected money from a bank in the Surrey commuter belt town of Banstead and finally drove down Sutton Lane towards London. Moody was a classic old-fashioned blagger, who knew that the success of all jobs lay in doing the groundwork, the necessary planning ahead of a heist.

The following day, Jimmy Moody met with gang leader Chopper Knight and the rest of the gang and told them about the van driver's precise movements. Then, a week before the scheduled robbery, the gang bought a van at a car auction and practised their chainsaw-cutting techniques in an abandoned garage in east London. Team member Bernie Khan, 34, later recalled: "It wasn't exactly the same kind of van, but it had similar metal sides. We knew how big the bags of money were, so we cut the holes just the right size. We'd thought about all this very carefully. We knew the van had an outside skin and once you got past that you got to the safe."

Then, in the days before the robbery, the gang meticulously organized the theft of seven "nicked-to-order" vehicles. They were moved around various locations in east and south London to make sure no one tracked them down. All the cars had been stolen using a special screwdriver with a barrel – known as a "donka". Bernie Khan recalled: "Chopper loved nickin' cars. It was all like a big chess game to him. Movin' them around from place to place, having his plan and sticking to it."

On the planned day of the heist, the team arrived in Banstead and found to their horror that the Security Express van driver was leaving the bank *an hour earlier than scheduled*. "It was just one of those things," explained Khan. "So we put it all on ice." Chopper Knight assured his gang this was nothing more than a temporary setback and immediately drew up a new set of plans to accommodate the time changes. "We'll still do it inside the next week," he told his men. Bernie Khan explained: "Chopper knew exactly what he was doing and we trusted him implicitly. He was the perfect pro."

On the morning of 15 August 1978, Jimmy Moody, Chopper Knight, Bernie Khan and the rest of the nine-man team of blaggers met at Moody's flat in Hackney, east London, which was the gang's "out" (safehouse) for the job. Knight gave his men a final briefing before they all left the flat separately – at one-minute intervals – to head for the stolen vehicles, parked in pre-designated spots within a few hundred yards of the flat.

Bernie Khan found himself driving a Ford Escort in a six-vehicle convoy as it headed across the river and into the south London suburbs en route to Banstead. Khan explained: "I was drivin' alone and wearing a boiler suit. I could see the boys in their motors in front and behind me. It was quite a turn-out, but we kept our distance from each other, so no one realized we were in convoy."

Then Khan was caught at a red traffic light. "Suddenly there's a siren and I see the police in my rear view mirror. I thought, 'Fuck it, my time's up. I'm gonna get a pull.'" Khan pulled his car over, got out and waited for the police to wave him down.

Khan's teammates saw what had happened and watched from a safe distance. "I had enough equipment on me to get convicted for goin' to rob," explained Khan. "I was a gonner."

But the police car floated right past Bernie Khan without giving him a second glance. "I couldn't fuckin' believe it," recalled Khan. "They didn't even look at me." It was a false alarm. Khan climbed back into the Escort and the robbers continued their journey.

The convoy spread out through the suburbs of south London to ensure it didn't spark any interest from other motorists. In some ways, recalled Khan, it was reminiscent of *The Italian Job*, except the gang was driving a cross section of Fords, Rovers and Jags instead of Minis. "The excitement and anticipation was building as we drove through south London. It was all part of the buzz, I guess," Khan later explained.

After two of the gang's vehicles had peeled off, the rest of the convoy stopped next to a small forest on the outskirts of

Banstead, on the Sutton Road, right in the heart of the semi-suburban Surrey countryside. Khan recalled: "We was early so we set the motors up in their right positions. We all knew what we had to do. No one needed to be told twice."

Over in nearby Banstead, two of the robber's vehicles were now shadowing the Security Express van from the moment it left the bank in the high street. Khan explained: "We picked it up at the bank at dead on 11. That was part of its schedule. We had a car in front and a car behind the van."

Less than a mile out of Banstead on the Sutton Road, the car in front of the security van put on its right indicator so that the van had to slow down. Khan explained: "Now the van's caught in the middle and having to slow down. Then another of our cars being driven by Jimmy Moody pulls out of a side turning to stop all the traffic behind the security van."

Just then the robbers' own mustard-yellow *Sherpa* van – covered in dents to make it look as if it had been in an accident – pulled out of another nearby lane and screeched to a halt alongside the Security Express vehicle. Three robbers with sawn-off shotguns emerged, surrounded the van and blew its tyres out with their weapons.

Khan recalled: "Then I jumped out with all our tools. We'd already warmed the chainsaw up earlier that morning, because sometimes they didn't start easily."

All the men were wearing flesh-coloured latex gloves and a variety of masks and helmets.

Gang leader Chopper Knight leapt out of a Ford Granada and stood to attention with a stopwatch in his hand.

Pressing the button firmly he announced: *"Three minutes, gentlemen."*

Chopper knew only too well they had to move very quickly and get all the cash out of that security van as quickly as possible. Perhaps surprisingly, Khan claims at least three of the robbers were not even armed. He later explained: "That wasn't our job. Jim and the others were the hired guns, not us."

On the other side of the Security Express van, gang member Sammy Benefield waved a sawn-off at the driver and his mate as he dragged them onto the grass verge. Benefield then leered over them with his weapon pointing menacingly down at them.

Team-leader Chopper Knight stood, arms folded, watching the entire proceedings, keeping an eye out for any unforeseen problems, his stopwatch clutched in his hand. "That clock of his was fuckin' tickin' away inside all our heads," recalled Khan.

Jimmy Moody – renowned for "having more front than Woolworths" – was dressed as a policeman holding up traffic and covering the back of the security van at the same time. Khan explained: "Jimmy could see behind us and in all directions. He was crucial. He'd know well in advance if anything or anybody was going to stumble upon us. He loved bein' the copper. He really got into the part."

By this time Khan had pulled his cutting goggles over his balaclava and he and gang member Tony Knightly got down to work. "We've got all the gear on," recalled Khan. "We look well professional and that fuckin' grinder is makin' a hell of a racket." Not surprisingly the security van staff looked terrified the moment Khan fired up his chainsaw. "Yeah it was a bit of a fearsome sight. We're cuttin' away and there's lots of smoke 'n' noise."

Many of the witnesses who were present when the Chainsaw Gang struck later recalled how frightening the noise of the cutter was above all else. One robbery victim said: "I'll never forget that noise as long as I live. It was horrible. It drowned out all other sounds and there was this feeling that they might turn the chainsaw on us if we dared to step out of line."

Bernie Khan recalls the Banstead job in almost reverential terms. His pride about the job matched only by his colourful language. "We had the whole road blocked off. It was masterful, a piece of art in a way. Everythin' went like clockwork." And the star of the show wasn't Khan, Moody, Knight or any of the rest of the team: it was that chainsaw ripping open the side of the security van like a sardine can.

"Those poor bastards looked fuckin' terrified as the chainsaw tore open the back of the van as if it was going through butter. Funny thing is, I reckon it must have sounded like tree felling out there in the countryside," added Khan.

Meanwhile, Moody the "policeman" continued ordering traffic to stop while the fearsome cutter continued tearing open the side of the Security Express van. Khan said: "Jim was standing there in his Old Bill uniform lookin' just the part. Only difference was he's got a pump (shotgun) under his arm. Wearin' that uniform was a brilliant idea 'cause it definitely impressed a lot of people. All them motorists just sat quietly. No one questioned us. Jim looked big and was holding that shooter (gun) like it was official."

"Two minutes, thirty seconds," bellowed Chopper Knight to his men.

Khan was still cutting away at the outer skin of the van. He explained: "The hole had to be big enough to get those money bags out. It was a precision cut and there was no point in holding back. We knew we only had a short amount of time."

Another gang member – John Segars – remained on lookout in the driver's seat of another back-up car parked alongside the security van. At that moment, one of the security-van guards tried to get up from the grass verge, where they'd been ordered to lie. Segars jumped from his vehicle and panned his sawn-off through the air.

"Don't fuckin' move!" he roared.

The van driver ignored the order.

Segars let off a warning shot and the driver dived back onto the ground.

"Two minutes!" screamed Chopper Knight, consulting his stopwatch and completely ignoring the incident. Despite the firing of the shotgun, the grinding noise of the chainsaw still dominated proceedings.

Khan explained: "That's when I finally got through the outer skin and was trying to bend it open so we could get into the cash. I remember turning to see if everything else was alright. It was a weird feeling because everything felt more vulnerable once the noise of the chainsaw stopped. There was a flatness in the air. I looked across and saw Jim still waving at the traffic jam behind us. What a fuckin' inspirational sight he was."

"One and a half!" shouted Knight.

Khan and Knightly then frantically began pulling the moneybags out of the van and transferring them straight into the robber's van. They later discovered that each bag contained £25,000.

As the last minute began counting down, the team upped the pace and formed a chain to get the bags out quicker. Khan recalled: "It just went on and on. We didn't realize there was so much fuckin' money in that van." Forty bags in total were thrown in the back of the robber's van.

They didn't realize it at the time, but they'd got more than four times the amount they'd originally expected.

Behind them, gang-member Jimmy Moody continued waving his sawn-off in the direction of an increasingly irate group of motorists.

"Go! Go! Go!" screamed Chopper, before blowing his football ref's whistle at full pelt just in case anyone hadn't heard him. The nine robbers piled into three vehicles, leaving three other cars behind.

And this is perhaps where their sheer professionalism showed up more than at any other time. Instead of screeching off in all directions, the gang moved off in their vehicles almost sedately, as if they didn't have a care in the world.

The gang was even careful not to exceed the 30mph speed limit as they drove away from the scene of the robbery. Khan explained: "We were keeping a low profile. Everyone was lookin' for motors screamin' up the road like they see on films. But we didn't do that. No one noticed us and we never even heard a siren."

The gang had earmarked a barn close to a nearby local hospital as the location at which they would swap vehicles.

Earlier, Chopper had even insisted the gang put their own padlock on the barn so no one else could get into it. Khan explained: "The motor was bumping around on a narrow lane. I'm sitting there opposite Segers and Benefield with Jim right at the back of the van. There were two others up front. Then we go over these sleepin' policemen and it got really bumpy."

Suddenly there was an almighty explosion.

Khan recalled: "This sawn-off in Segars's hand went off and the shot skimmed my ear leaving a huge fuckin' hole in the side of the van."

There was stunned silence in the back of the van as Khan and Segars looked at each other.

"What the fuckin' hell you doin'?" asked Khan.

Segars looked embarrassed and clambered into the front of the van without uttering a word.

Khan insisted: "I was nearly killed by John Segars. No two ways about it. If I'd been further away the shot would have spread and finished me off."

The robbers' first vehicle then nudged open the gates to a field just ahead of their drop point at the barn. Segars jumped out and shut the gate behind them before they headed down a dirt track. At the barn, they transferred their loot into three stolen Fords before heading back into London.

Less than half an hour later, robber Jimmy Moody was driving a metallic green Granada with fellow gang member Segars sitting alongside him as they moved swiftly through the suburbs of south London. In the boot were sack-loads of money, guns and their infamous chainsaw. Segars ducked down when a police car with its siren going and blue light flashing passed in the opposite direction. Segars later recalled: "My fuckin' bottle went when I saw that cop car and I told Jim." Moody was appalled by what he saw as Segars' cowardly behaviour and ordered him out of the car to cool down. He told Segars to meet the gang at the "out" later that afternoon.

Segars went into the nearest pub, bought a large brandy and a pint of bitter. When he put his hand into his pocket to pay for the drinks he felt a spent cartridge case, which he'd earlier put in his pocket after discharging it during the robbery. Segars immediately went to the pub toilet and hid it in the cistern.

Later that same evening, at 6pm, 40 bags of cash containing a total of almost £800,000 were carried up to Moodys' flat at 38 Lexfield Court, Pownall Road, in Hackney, in a plastic body bag with a zipper down the front. Khan recalled: "We arrived in the three motors and lugged the cash up the stairs over our shoulders. We were all fuckin' knackered. The old buzz had long since gone."

When gang member Segars turned up with his Saluki dog to claim his share, he was immediately told by dog-hater Moody to "fuck off and come back without yer mutt". Jimmy Moody hated Segars more by the minute and had no doubt he was a potential grass.

It was only then that gang leader Knight discovered the team had left at least five bags in the van still parked outside. Two gang members were distpatched to bring it in. After they returned, Knight ordered the team to strip to their underpants to avoid leaving any forensic clues on their clothing or in the flat. Even at that point none of the gang realized they'd actually just stolen close to a million pounds, worth at least 20 times that amount today.

Then the count began. In deadly silence, Knight began stacking bundles of notes up in a corner of the room. Within ten minutes he'd counted so much cash that Benefield and Khan were sent out to a shop up the road to buy holdalls because the kitbags they had weren't big enough to hold each robber's share of the money.

Khan later vividly described the scene in the flat that day: "Each room had been cleared of furniture and Chopper had made piles of the money and packed them into plastic parcels, each with £25,000. It was completely fuckin' unreal. I kept pinchin' meself to remind me that this was pure cash."

When "dodgy" John Segars returned, he was also ordered to take off his clothes. He later explained: "I didn't know what the fuck they were on about at first. It all sounded a bit dodgy, but then Chopper explained and I started stripping off. The whole team were in their vests, sweating like bullocks, counting the bundles of notes into separate piles."

Each share came to exactly £96,000.

One of the gang later said: "There was just thousands upon thousands of notes stacked up in neat little piles on the bare floor. The money was everywhere, inches deep on the floor."

Khan had other memories of that afternoon: "You know those films where they're thowin' the money up into the air? You know what? That's so fuckin' unreal. This was the opposite. Really low key. None of that movie bollocks. All Chopper kept saying was, 'There's still a lot more to do yet.'"

As Segars was leaving the flat clutching his holdall full of cash, Chopper Knight asked him for £300 he'd loaned him some months earlier when he was broke.

"Fuck off, Chopper," replied Segars.

"I want that fuckin' £300 or you don't leave here," said Knight, rising to his feet.

Jimmy Moody also stood up with a gun clutched in the palm of his hand.

"D'you want some of this?" he said to Segars, not even bothering to look down at the gun.

Another gang member in the flat recalled: "So John had to pay up before he was allowed to leave. It was a heavy moment and I've no doubt Moody would have done him if Chopper had given him the go-ahead. Moody fuckin' hated John anyway."

The entire transaction at Jimmy Moody's flat – including handing the money to each gang member – took just 20 minutes. Khan recalled: "We all got it into our zip-ups and got out one at a time. I put my money in the boot of my motor and away I went to my flop in north London where I put the money in a safe, put my feet up and sat watching telly. I didn't go out for days."

On the afternoon of 15 August 1978, Operation Ohio detective Bill Forman got a call from Surrey Police to say a gang had just used a chainsaw to prize open a Security Express van.

He believed the Chainsaw Gang had been throwing down the gauntlet ever since they first started their blaggings. But now it felt personal. "It was their way of saying: 'Come and get us if you can,'" Forman later recalled.

The first senior police investigator on the scene in Banstead was Detective Chief Superintendent Jim Sewell of the Robbery Squad. He was full of admiration for the robber's skills. "It was very unusual, well planned, really an old-fashioned Dick Turpin/Robin Hood-type robbery using motor cars and sophisticated equipment," he told one reporter.

That evening a very tired and weary Bill Forman left Banstead police station after examining the attack vehicles and hearing descriptions of the robbers. He believed it was now only a matter of time before one of the Chainsaw Gang's victims died. He needed to bring them to justice immediately. The robbery also sent shockwaves through the security industry. It forced banks to find better ways of protecting their cash. Naturally the robbery was such an audacious crime that it also drew admiring comments from many in the London underworld.

One legendary robber from that era later recalled: "This was pure art. The Chainsaw Gang synchronized their entire blagging like true pros. In London, we all felt a twinge of admiration for them. They had front, courage and sheer determination combined with very good inside knowledge. It looked to many of us that they could dominate the robbery scene for many years to come."

Just a week after the Banstead job, a notorious London criminal called Mickey Calvey (now deceased) told detectives that Chainsaw Gang member John Segars had been one of the eight robbers on that heist. Detective Bill Forman eventually tracked down Segars, who immediately announced: "Fuck it! I've had enough."

Within days of his arrest, he'd named all the other members of the Chainsaw Gang and gradually, one by one, they were all tracked down, arrested and charged. All except Jimmy Moody, who always seemed to be one step ahead of the law and who managed to avoid arrest for a long period after his fellow blaggers had been nicked.

AFTERMATH

In November 1979, the Chainsaw Gang members – except on-the-run robber Jimmy Moody – were jailed for a total of 218 years at Maidstone Crown Court. Before sentencing gang leader Chopper Knight to 18 years, Judge Justice Stocker told him: "I have not the slightest doubt you were the leader – and a very good one, too. You would have been the leader in any field you chose to follow. You chose this one. You are a very dangerous man. These robberies of which you have been convicted showed a high degree of organization and extremely careful planning and execution."

Later the same judge told the gang as a whole: "You all possess qualities which would have fitted you as leaders among fellow men. You are all extremely intelligent with abilities of organization and planning and you all possess courage. It's tragic that you used these qualities to make war on us."

On-the-run Jimmy Moody was furious at the length of the sentences handed down to his associates, but he reserved the most-venom for two robbers he believed had turned informants in order to get shorter sentences. Moody told one associate: "I'd fuckin' do 'em for nothin'. Free of charge!"

Moody was eventually hunted down and surrounded by dozens of police – led by Detective Bill Forman – at a secret hideout in south London. Moody surrendered to avoid a firefight. He then wrote a full confession of his involvement with the Chainsaw Gang, but before his case went to court, Moody was on the run once more following a daring breakout from London's Brixton Prison, where he escaped with an IRA terrorist and another well-known London criminal.

Yet, as Bill Forman told me many years later, time had been running out for the Chainsaw Gang ever since what most villains and police officers agree was the team's most spectacular robbery in London's busy Blackwall Tunnel on 29 September 1977. It convinced hard-working police detective Forman that he could not rest until he'd brought them to justice. This robbery was a particularly huge boost to blagger Jimmy Moody's reputation because it was the first time he dressed up as a policeman to hold back the traffic, which brought this reaction from a lawyer who later defended him in court: "Those were the days when an awful lot of policemen came from the same background as the villains they were chasing. It was hard to tell the Flying Squad guy and the armed robber apart, and Jim made a very plausible copper!"

In the Blackwall Tunnel raid, "PC" Moody created a gap in the traffic and forced a security van to stop just past the bend about two-thirds of the way into the tunnel. At the same time, two of the robbers staged a crash behind them to block the tunnel just before the bend. The gang used three stolen cars and a stolen van to surround the security wagon. The team had done their homework, because the security van's radio was useless once the van was inside the tunnel.

"PC" Moody then leapt out of his car, "confiscated" the keys of several motorists behind them in the tunnel at gunpoint so they couldn't drive off and raise the alarm. The underworld loved such subtle, dramatic touches. There were even rumours a detective had provided the police uniforms for the job, as well as talk of other officers being given "payoffs" from the takings of the Blackwall Tunnel job to ensure the robbers weren't apprehended.

Three of the gang had been armed with sawn-off shotguns, one with a pistol and another with an axe, which was used to smash the security van window to force the crew to co-operate. But what few villains mentioned in the middle of all these legendary tales was that robber Moody attacked the custodian of the money and felled him with a shotgun butt during the job. He was so badly injured that he ended up drawing a disability pension.

The transfer of the money into the getaway vehicle had to be done with precise timing because the longer it took, the more likely the police would arrive and nobody wanted a shootout. One robber described the Blackwall Tunnel job like this: "As we got into the back of the security van I asked myself why was I putting myself through all this shit? Nerves, fear, excitement, all combined. Earlier, the worse period had been waitin' for the van that you're gonna rob to turn up. You think everyone's lookin' at you, because you're standin' around on a warm day with gloves on. One finger print and you've had it. But once the job started it was fuckin' beautiful. It was a feelin' I can't put into words. First my eyes went watery and supersensitive to light. Then I got that little *ping* and that's when it really all kicked in; that feelin' of complete and utter invinciblity. Then the security vehicle – the target – finally turned up. All of a sudden we're in for the kill. The minute you go for it your body relaxes. It's happenin'. At that moment I felt so strong I could have picked up that van and run along the road with it. Next thing you're lookin inside that bag at the cash and that's fuckin' beautiful."

The gang escaped from the Blackwall Tunnel that day with almost £100,000 in wage packets destined for the Greenwich group of hospitals. Only a small fraction of that cash was ever recovered. Once the money was divided up at a flophouse within hours of the crime being committed, the team simply went their separate ways.

After escaping with the IRA man from Brixton jail, Jimmy Moody was never caught. But in June 1993, his life on the run came to an end when he was shot dead by an unnamed assailant as he supped on a pint in a pub on the edge of Victoria Park, in east London.

Some believe that the cold-blooded hit on Moody marked the end of an era…

4. SNOW OVER SHOREDITCH

"It's all about the planning. You don't just pick a place and rob it. You watch it and wait for the right moment. You clock all the activity. You know who is going in and out. Even down to when the fuckin' milkman comes."

Freddie Foreman

City of London, Good Friday, April 1983

Snow at Easter is virtually unheard of in Britain, so when the country got blanketed in the stuff on the evening of Good Friday, 1983, it made the front pages of all the newspapers and was the lead story on every TV news bulletin. As legendary villain Freddie Foreman told me recently: "The air was as crisp as a £5 note."

But then he should know, because Foreman, 51, was one of five men hiding inside a giant dustbin in the yard of the Security Express money depot in Shoreditch, on the edge of London's financial district, the City, or the "Golden Square

Mile" as it is often called. The other four men were Ronnie Knight, 49 (the actress Barbara Windsor's now ex-husband), his brother John, 43, Terry Perkins and Ronnie Everett.

That un-seasonal snowstorm was just about the only thing the blaggers hadn't planned for. As Foreman explained: "We prided ourselves on being thorough professionals. This was a piece of work to us, nothing more, nothing less." And there seems little doubt that the notorious Foreman and his "team" of London "old pros" aimed to show the underworld a thing or two about the Art of Robbery.

After months of careful, detailed reconnaissance work, the gang had specifically chosen a quiet Bank Holiday weekend to pull off what they believed would be the Crime of the Century. As Foreman explained: "We was on top of our game at that time. I s'ppose we felt invincible in many ways."

But Foreman and his team were no amateurs. They'd all emerged from the London crime scene of the 1960s dominated by the Krays and Richardsons. Old-time professional villains from a time when gangsters helped old ladies across the street and who would come down like a ton of bricks on anyone who harmed women and children in their community.

Today, with the streets of the UK filled with many cold-blooded foreign criminals, it's hard to imagine that, not so long ago, characters like Foreman and his accomplices were the "hardcore" of British criminality.

And the key to their professionalism was in the "research". Foreman explained to me: "It's all research. We weren't smash-and-grab merchants. We needed a window to operate within. It took months of watching."

The heavily fortified Security Express redbrick complex

had 12-foot-high walls and steel-shuttered doors plus alarms and CCTV cameras placed around the entire perimeter. The team had even carefully pinpointed a section of the perimeter wall that was a blind spot to the overhanging CCTV cameras.

So, silently, like human cats, the five robbers slipped over the wall into the yard of the depot on that Good Friday, convinced that they could then wait inside this fortress for the entire weekend, if necessary, until the right moment to pounce arrived.

Foreman explained: "We'd found that 'blind spot' by waiting and watching. And then we chose the perfect time to go over the wall. We'd first thought about going over the loading bay and nick all the bags off a van that way… We'd watched it for ages to get the hang of what was happening. We'd done a similar system in a couple of previous Post Office robberies."

But then it became clear there was a lot more cash on site if the robbers picked a holiday weekend and decided to go inside the actual building.

"We'd watched with binoculars from across the road where we had the perfect lookout post. We took it in turns through the night and day. We'd waited for a chink in their armour – the moment when we knew the place was vulnerable and that we could get in."

The gang had used a derelict office block to watch the premises of the country's leading security firm for several months. "That was a real stroke of luck. Looking back on it now I can't quite believe how Security Express didn't work out what a perfect spot that was for any blaggers wanting to watch them."

It became clear to the robbers during the reconnaissance "stage" that they could steal much more if they showed patience and professionalism, something Freddie Foreman had bucket-loads of.

"In a way the job just grew and grew. We all knew that if we were patient and waited for the perfect moment then we'd get ten times more than we had originally expected," explained Foreman.

So it was that the gang had calculated that the vaults would be overflowing with five tons of cash in silver and paper money over this Bank Holiday weekend. Britain under Margaret Thatcher was swimming in *readies* and Freddie Foreman and his associates reckoned Security Express was the nearest thing to their own twisted version of a "Fort Knox".

So on that icy cold Good Friday evening, Foreman and the four other men shivered away in that massive black plastic dustbin as they waited for dawn to break.

At almost 4am, the men broke their self-imposed silence to exchange a few words. The floor beneath them was ice-cold and, as on every public holiday weekend, the City of London was deserted. Only the noise of distant goods trains rumbling along a track at Liverpool Street station broke the dead, snow-blinded silence. It was exactly what they had hoped for.

Most robberies are severly restricted by time. As Foreman later explained: "Usually you have a couple of minutes to get in and out, but on this one we just sat back and waited until the perfect moment. It almost felt as if we had too much time our hands."

The men didn't say much during that 4am exchange before falling back into silence. After weeks of going through all the plans for the job their heads were buzzing. Escape routes had been mapped out, vehicles assembled and a flophouse located. If the gang all kept to their pre-arranged script then the job couldn't fail. But as Foreman explained: "In this game you never count yer chickens. There will always be something unexpected that occurs and you have to be ready to deal with it instantly."

It wasn't until three hours later – at 7am – that the door to the building opened and a guard called Greg Counsell took over from the duty nightshift man. Inside the main office of the depot, Counsell poured himself some hot water from a kettle into a cup before realizing that he had to go outside to get the milk. "We'd watched him get it loads of times before. We knew that this was our opportunity to get into the building.

"Everything had been dependent on that milk being delivered earlier," continued Foreman. "When we'd heard the crates rattling on the electric milk cart it cheered us up. We hoped this guy was on his own in there and that he'd come to get the milk and unlock all the doors into the depot to get that milk. That would be our chance."

Foreman continued: "He had to come out of the building to get the milk and that meant unlocking several doors to get to the back door and open the back door and then get across the yard to the little control box which he had to go into. It had a dog flap where they put the bottle of milk.

"Once inside it, he grabbed the bottle of milk and locked up the dog box/office where they open and control the electric doors. They were big folding doors all operated from switches. Normally there was someone else in that box, but at this time of the morning there was no one there."

The noise of the huge ring of keys jangling against Greg Counsell's thigh with every step got louder and louder as he continued unlocking door after door. As he had done many times before, Counsell presumed he was safe and had left all the doors open behind him as he went through the various sealed corridors towards the outside door where the milk would be sitting in the specially built hub.

"He came out, walked across the yard, got the milk. We knew he then had to come out. He'd left the back door open to come across the yard and that was our moment to strike," Foreman explained.

As the firm heard the heavy bolt slide open on the outside door, they knew it was time…

When Counsell opened the door he came face to face with a masked man brandishing a sawn-off shotgun.

"He immediately stepped away from the door after seeing my mate pointing the shotgun at him. That was stupid. We shouldn't have waved the gun at him as he came through the door at that stage, because Counsell naturally panicked and tried to shut the door on us."

Foreman continued: "Counsell stood back. I don't blame him. You see a shotgun when you open a door and, of course, you're fuckin' going to slam it shut. That was plain stupid. You have to let them get out before you show them the shooter. But luckily he left that door open."

The robbers were so "pumped up" for action, they raced into the building through the open doorways. Foreman opened the final glass door of the main reception area and the gang swept in. Two wore monkey masks and the rest of the gang members were in balaclavas. All had on boiler suits and gloves and were tooled up – armed. No wonder Counsell took the sensible route and immediately co-operated.

"We didn't know for sure if there were any more staff in the building. The others ran in the door to see if anyone else was in there while I shouted at Counsell: 'Who else is in there?' He said, 'No one. No one,' and he was telling the truth. 'I'm on me own,' he said. So I knew we were going to be okay. It was a dream come true.

"The doors were all unlocked and we had a free run at it. All the offices were upstairs. I knew that once we had Counsell in our custody we had control of everything."

But this was only just the beginning of the Big Job. Now the gang would have to wait patiently for more than six hours while the rest of the staff drifted in because they had the keys and relevant codes to open three of the main underground vaults. A further seven guards were due to turn up that afternoon and each of them had to be taken care of one by one.

"Just keep your head down as if you're reading the newspaper and it'll all be fine," Foreman told Counsell as he "prepped" him for the arrival of his workmates.

Foreman ordered Counsell to read the newspaper and "pretend nothing is happening". He explained: "I told him to look at the newspaper and not anywhere else because I knew when his workmates saw his eyes they'd see the fear in them. Your eyes tell everything."

"You know what? I've never forgotten to this day how the

corridor and ground floor of the place was like being back in the nick with that series of locked doors we needed to get through."

"Counsell somehow managed to 'act normal' as each of his workmates arrived at the depot," Foreman continued. "He opened the doors for his workmates. As he answered, each one walked in and waited at the other end of the corridor where the entrance was. I said, 'Don't fucking look at anyone' and he did as he was told, but the phone kept ringing all the fucking time and he had to answer it and I am listening to every word he says.

"Lots of supermarkets and other clients were calling up to find out where the vans had got to. 'When you coming to collect our cash?' they were asking. I told Counsell to tell them all that the vans were having mechanical problems and they would be along as soon as possible.

"I had never allowed for this and my reaction was completely off the cuff and thank Christ it worked. Then Counsell's wife called up to ask him to pick up some shopping on the way home later. Fuckin' shopping she wanted! He was shakin' like a leaf, but he did a good job."

And between each member of staff turning up, Counsell had to face the full wrath of fearsome Freddie Foreman.

"He kept saying, 'Don't hurt me. Don't hurt me.' I said, 'Listen to me Greg, you ain't gonna get hurt as long as you do what I fuckin' tell you. Don't do anythin' wrong. Don't do anythin' stupid or silly. Okay? You'll lose yer fuckin' bollocks if you do anythin' stupid.'"

Foreman went on: "You have to frighten them, but not so much that they can't do what you need them to do. It's a fine balance and it's part of the art of a robbery… a terrified bloke is no good to me…"

Eventually Counsell let in every staff member.

Foreman explained: "I was sitting behind bulletproof glass near Counsell as each staff member came in. But from where I was sitting, he could easily have run off and probably got away from us if he'd had the bottle. Thank God he didn't.

"Then he would have got to the street and started screaming his head off and there wouldn't have been a thing we could do about it. I mean, we can't just follow him out there and sort him can we? It was a good thing it was a Bank Holiday because there weren't so many people around. But if someone had run out, we'd have had to leave them.

"Mind you, that had happened to me before on another job. This punter went running out in the road shouting and screaming 'Robbery. The bank's been robbed.' It was a nightmare for us and I was desperate to make sure it didn't happen again on this job."

Foreman himself doesn't refer to it, but as Counsell's colleagues arrived one of them, 61-year-old guard James Alcock, was doused in petrol and had a box of matches rattled by his ear with the threat that he would be "incinerated" if he failed to hand over the keys needed to gain access to the vaults.

Foreman, who was acting as "gatekeeper" as the workforce arrived, explained: "As each staff member came in they were copped by us at the other end of that corridor. We had the guns pointed at them. None argued. We tied them up, made them comfortable by putting coats behind their heads and even gave their legs a massage and turned them over so they didn't get pins and needles. I even offered them cigarettes and held them for them while they inhaled them.

"Then I offered them a cup of tea. I mean, we was with them for best part of eight hours. It was a bloody long time and we needed to keep them all in good shape. We had no intention of harming them as long as they played ball.

"We needed them to be in decent health. It wasn't in our interests to hurt them. We wanted them fit and healthy. No point in them panicking, because then they was no use to us. We weren't there to hurt anyone. We were there to do some business, simple as that. We just wanted them to lay down and not give us any aggro."

One by one the guards were wrapped up in women's stockings and a plaster was put over their mouths. Now it was time to open the vaults. The team knew only too well that one incorrect turn of a key or a code put in wrongly and the bells in the building's alarm system would literally ring.

"But it went as smooth as silk and hey presto! The doors opened and there was all the cash we'd expected, just staring back at us," recalls Foreman. "What a magic feeling that was!"

With the vault doors open, the Firm transferred the cash onto trolleys and sent them up on a lift to the loading bays, where a seven-ton truck was waiting. Each sack they moved along a human chain contained £100,000.

After more than eight hours on the premises, the gang eventually had packed bundles of bank notes in denominations of £50 downwards totalling £5,961,097 into their waiting getaway van.

"Get in! Get in!" yelled one of the gang after they had

emptied the vault of almost every last pound.

It was time for the escape.

Moments later the van moved across the yard and started to pick up speed as it cleared the narrow entrance gate with ease. The rest of the gang followed on foot, dispersing casually as they headed to their getaway vehicles that were parked in the surrounding streets.

As the gates to the depot were closing, one remaining gang member squeezed through the gap having been almost left behind when he found himself lost for breath moments earlier in the yard. Relieved, the last man standing – as he was to become known to all the gang – jumped into a car being driven by another member of the gang and they then pulled away.

Foreman recalled: "The van was so full of fuckin' money when we left there that one of the team had to climb on top of the cash and lie on it – seriously.

"Afterwards that guy literally smelled of money. You see we only had so many cars, so we had to make do with what we had to get everyone away from there very quickly. We had an outside man moving all the cars around so no one spotted them. There was a market nearby and we had to make sure all our cars were ready and available when we wanted them. We didn't want to find that they had been towed away or anything like that. All the cars were ringers – stolen. But they were a vital part of the operation."

Thanks to the freezing temperatures, there was little traffic on the Bank Holiday roads. So the Firm, all of them driving in their separate vehicles, slipped through the quiet London streets with ease. There was no celebration inside the main van. Not yet. Instead the entire firm sat quiet, still alert. The only noise was the sound of the windscreen wipers as the snow continued falling.

The next step of the job was to count the money in the flophouse.

Foreman explained: "That was a surreal sight. All that cash just laid out in so many piles you couldn't see the carpet underneath. A lot of it was in £50 notes. Everything in there had to be counted. But we didn't cut it up. I just took my third away. The others took five sacks of money into a lock-up garage, which had been hired before the job."

The idea was to disperse all the millions of pounds of used notes very gradually so as to not alert the authorities. But laundering five tons of stolen banknotes was no easy task. It might have taken criminal genius to commit the robbery, but the hardest part of the job would be getting away with it.

Freddie Foreman's overwhelming memory of the flophouse "stage" of the robbery was the *buzz*. "It was an incredible feeling. Fuckin' hell! We'd just got away with it and now we were in a safe environment for the first time since going over that wall. It's indescribable."

Foreman says he carefully counted his share and "then we had to compare the other two parts, and if everyone was happy we could then get going. We had to have exactly the same. We knew what it should be. God that was a feeling. We had done it! We'd got away with it. What a rush."

A few hours later, the gang made their first, fatal error. As one of the robbers, John Knight, was coming out of the lock-up where some of the cash had been taken, someone saw him and said, "Oh, that's Barbara Windsor's brother-in-law." "That was it," said Foreman. "We was fucked after that because people remember things like that.

"Everything started to go downhill from that moment onwards. Talk about bad luck. This cunt was supposed to look after the money in the lock-up, but as soon as the team left, this bastard went in there and nicked five grand. Arsehole. Then another bloke nicked £360,000 and put it in his father-in-law's wardrobe in the council flat.

"And the idiot was also writing all his sums in relation to the money on the back of the door in the council flat and when the police found it they used it as evidence. It was all there written down. He had £360,000 and kept a tally of all the deductions.

"The lock-up was a little building with garages and, you know what? The police didn't even know the money from the robbery was there until they stumbled on it. Can you believe that? They originally thought it was an amphetamine factory because they'd found a van that had been used by a drug dealer nearby."

Then all the cards started falling. Foreman explained: "The cops got onto a pub run by our 'car man' and they even claimed some of the money was hidden there. I don't know if that's true, but it probably was."

Foreman remains angry to this day that the "car man" was not properly paid for his role in the robbery. "That was out of order. He was an important part of the team. Just 'cos he didn't go on the actual robbery doesn't take away from the importance of his role. He got nicked the same as everyone else as well."

AFTERMATH

Foreman, Ronnie Knight and the other robbery team members, Ronnie Everett, Clifford Saxe and John Mason, immediately fled to southern Spain where they inspired the "Costa del Crime" phrase because back then there was no extradition treaty between the UK and Spain, which enabled British crooks to live openly in the sun. The Security Express gang members who hid out in Spain became known as "The Famous Five".

Foreman was eventually "kidnapped" by Scotland Yard police officers and flown back to London in handcuffs to face trial for the Security Express job. Foreman was jailed for nine years in 1990. He believes that the door with the takings from the robbery written on it was one of the police's pivotal pieces of evidence.

"They used that door as evidence at my trial and even brought it into court as an exhibit. They laid it in front of me and the jury. They totted it all up. The cops even thought that the £360,000 was an exact share of the robbery and that 23 people took part in it. They thought it was a share, but that just wasn't true."

Ronnie Knight finally returned to Britain in 1995 to be sentenced for his role in the Security Express job.

Today, Foreman takes a philosophical view of the Security Express job aftermath. "It was overshadowed by Brink's-Mat because it happened so soon after that, but it was a fine, professional job… the Brink's boys didn't even realize what was in that warehouse. Talk about being lucky! Luck. That's still the key in this game."

Foreman concluded: "Overall I look back on that job as a good bit of work. No one got injured. No one had to go to hospital. We got what we wanted and the staff were unharmed. What more do you want?"

It's not quite the full truth, but a fair reflection of one of the most professional, perfectly executed robberies ever committed in Britain in the last century.

5. Men on a Mission

"I'm feeling much better now. It's like a weight off my mind. It was just too big. I couldn't handle it. There's one thing though. I'm worried about these people, what they're going to do to me..."

Inside man Tony Black's confession to police

Hounslow, West London, 26 November 1983, 6.25am

Only CCTV cameras and spotlights mounted on the walls of Unit 7, a steel-and-brick-built box on a scruffy trading estate near London's Heathrow Airport, caught the attention of curious onlookers. But when the huge orange-and-white armoured shutter doors rolled open, the building's real purpose was revealed. Chunky dark-blue Brink's-Mat vans, with barred and tinted black windows, came and went from the well-protected loading bay – day and night. Unit 7 wasn't Fort Knox or the Bank of England, but it did hold one of Britain's biggest safes, used to store currency, precious metals and other high-risk consignments often en route to the nearby airport.

It was still pitch black and icy cold on the morning of Saturday, 26 November 1983 as the early shift of workers waited outside kicking their heels, blowing clouds of mist while waiting for the 6.30am "opening time" to arrive. That was when the automatic timer would neutralize the sophisticated alarm system, allowing the keys to be inserted without triggering flashing lights, bells and alarms linked to the local police station and other security companies.

Security guard Richard Holliday had been the first to arrive in his beige Ford Consul. Another guard, Ron Clarke, quickly followed him on his moped. Guards Peter Bentley and Robin Riseley then pulled up moments later, and the four men mumbled greetings to one another. The fifth guard roistered for duty was nervy Tony Black, 31. Typically, he was late and still hadn't arrived when supervisor Michael Scouse, 37, drove up. Scouse, a former Special Constable, was the longest-serving member of staff on duty that day, with 12 years on the Brink's-Mat payroll. His seniority singled him out that morning as the "keyman".

Scouse entered the unit alone and locked the door behind him, leaving the crew outside while he went to a downstairs office and collected the key from the safe. This switched off the alarm system covering the perimeter walls and windows.

Scouse then went back to the main door to allow the rest of the crew in. The outside door was relocked from the inside before Scouse reactivated the alarm system, climbed the stairs and walked through to the radio-control room to look through the paperwork for the day's duties. Meanwhile, the other four guards went into the rest room to take off their coats. Holliday paused briefly to switch on the radio-room aerials and the surveillance cameras before joining his mates. Just then the doorbell rang. The guards heard Scouse go downstairs to let in guard Tony Black, who was ten minutes late.

"You look a bit rough," quipped guard Bentley as Black walked into the rest room. Black did indeed look pale, unkempt and apprehensive, as if he had just clambered out of bed and raced to work; he confirmed Bentley's suspicion that he had overslept, then, mumbling something about having to use the toilet, he disappeared downstairs again.

Guard Riseley glanced at his watch. It was 6.40am.

Brian Robinson, 38, Mickey McAvoy, 29, Tony White, 36, Brian Perry, 45, George Francis, 43, and John Lloyd, 42, were sitting in a stolen blue Transit van on the Heathrow trading estate, waiting for their "inside man" Tony Black (Robinson's brother-in-law) to give them the signal. Black would then let them into the Brink's-Mat warehouse where, the gang had been told, there were goods worth up to £3 million. Thanks to Tony Black, the robbers even already knew which of the two security guards had the combination numbers to allow access to the safes.

Black hadn't gone to the toilet. Instead, he had made his way to the front door to let in McAvoy and his gang.

Brink's-Mat's so-called state-of-the-art vault was protected by nothing more than a single, fixed surveillance camera attached to the building, but it was on the opposite side to the main door. There was an alarm on the door, which sounded when the gang members pushed their way in, but no one could possibly hear it upstairs, nor was it connected to anything outside the trading estate.

"Get on the floor or you're fuckin' dead."

The masked figure filling the doorway of the restroom spat out the words in a harsh Cockney accent, motioning urgently to the stunned guards with a 9mm Browning automatic. Riseley dived from his chair to the floor, quickly followed by Clarke and Holliday.

"The first thing I knew," recalled Robin Riseley, the guard who, along with Scouse, had the combination numbers, "was a man pointing a semi-automatic pistol at my face and telling us all to hit the floor."

On the floor, Riseley caught a brief glimpse of a white man, about 5 feet 8 inches tall and clean shaven, wearing a trilby hat and a dark car coat or anorak over a black blazer, black trousers and a black tie. But for the yellow balaclava that covered all but his eyes he might have been dressed for a funeral.

For a tense beat or two nothing happened. Someone later called it a hesitant silence. Then the gunman with the Browning automatic made a move that was to earn him the nickname "The Bully" among the guards. Without a word, he jerked his weapon arm upwards and – a silver blazer button glinting in the neon light – smashed the weapon down on the back of guard Peter Bentley's neck.

The guard had angered him by being slow to react when the door first crashed open and, believing it to be a colleague playing one of their regular practical jokes, Bentley stood by the sink continuing to make the tea. After being hit, Bentley's head hit the table as he crashed to the floor, dazing him momentarily and opening up two deep, bloody gashes in his scalp. The attacker's gun arm then calmly beckoned through the open door to someone waiting outside, and another three more robbers rushed into the room.

"Lie still and be fuckin' quiet," ordered The Bully, as his henchmen began to immobilize the terrified guards, pulling their arms behind their backs and handcuffing them, before locking their legs together at the shins with heavy-duty tape. Cloth bags with strings were then pulled down over the guard's heads and fastened around their necks.

One of the other guards was close enough to the gunman to distinguish the herringbone pattern of the tweed hat and the crispness of his starched white shirt. He even saw a lock of fair hair protruding from the balaclava as the bag was placed over his head.

Guard Bentley felt hands roughly pulling at the house and car keys on his belt. Then his watch was snatched off and thrown across the room. Blood from his throbbing head trickled down his face and neck. A moment later a voice, sounding almost sympathetic, asked if he was okay. Bentley nodded and the drawstring was loosened a little.

Meanwhile, guard Holliday was finding it difficult to breathe. Thrashing about on the floor, he attracted the attention of one of the robbers, who bent down and untied the drawstring, pulling the bag back to clear his upper lip. To ease the discomfort further, he was turned on his back. Guard Ron Clarke was similarly treated; first roughly bound and then casually asked if he was in any distress.

Moments later another robber spoke – this time with no discernible accent – and barked out orders. "Get that radio tuned in. If you hear anything, tell us," he barked to one of the other robbers. The guards immediately realized that this man was the commanding "officer".

Seconds later several of the robbers left the room. Then a radio crackled through frequencies as it tuned in to a Metropolitan Police wavelength. There was precious little happening outside the Brink's-Mat warehouse: two police officers could be heard discussing a spot-check on a vehicle, but nothing else. Two members of the gang then returned and hauled Holliday to his feet before dragging him down the corridor into the locker room.

He was then lowered to the floor and pushed back against a girder. They tried to handcuff him to the steel strut, but failed because it was too large for his arms to encircle. He was handcuffed to a radiator instead.

Fellow guard Ron Clarke was then also hauled in and handcuffed to the same radiator. They were left alone to listen to the noises echoing in the vault directly below them.

Senior guard Scouse was pulled to his feet in the rest room and dragged outside into the corridor, where he was thrown against a wall.

"Breathe in," ordered one of the robbers.

Scouse felt his shirt pulled up to his chin and then a hand tugged violently at his waistband.

"Breathe in deeply or you'll get fuckin' cut." Just then the knife sliced through his belted jeans from the buckle to the crotch. As Scouse filled his lungs, he became aware of an overpowering smell. A rag had been waved under his nose.

Tony Black had earlier identified Scouse and Riseley to the robbers as the men who held the combinations. Their ordeal was about to begin in earnest.

Risely recalled: "They slipped a hood on my head and then there was a knife in the crotch of my trousers and before I could say anything they were down round my ankles and there was a liquid being poured on me."

Scouse recalled: "I heard this voice say, 'If we don't get what we want, if the police turn up or the alarms go off I'll…"

Then the voice stopped momentarily.

"D'you recognize that smell?" asked one gang member.

The same robber – later indentified as Mickey McAvoy – then poured petrol into Scouse's lap.

Scouse instantly felt the fuel seeping into his genitals and stinging his skin.

"You'd better do as fuckin' I say, or I'll put a match to the petrol and a bullet through your fuckin' head," said McAvoy. "I know you live in a flat in Ruislip High Street above a TV rental shop. We've been watching you for nine months and setting this up for 12. Now, let's get on with it. You have two numbers."

The two guards were taken down to the vault, which they believed held a million pounds in used banknotes. Scouse punched in his half of the combination, but when Riseley was pushed forward to complete the sequence there was a problem. Riseley later recalled: "The company had just changed the combinations and I hadn't memorized the new one, so the safe wouldn't open. They felt I was messing about.

I heard someone say: 'It looks like we've got a hero,' and he started rattling a matchbox in front of my face. He then pulled out a diver's knife and said he was going to castrate me if I didn't give him the numbers. He was furious. Well, I was doing my best."

After 20 minutes of trying and failing to break into the safe, the robbers, almost by default, turned their attention to the drums and boxes scattered around the floor of the vault. As they opened the various lids and discovered scrap silver, degraded platinum and highly traceable traveller's cheques, it seemed the job was going to end in disappointment.

With a gun in his back, Scouse finally coughed up the numbers. After they had been punched in, he looked over his shoulder and declared that the alarms were now neutralized. The robbers were finally inside Unit 7's vault.

It was shortly before 7am and the fluorescent lighting had revealed nothing more than a carpet of drab grey containers, no bigger than shoeboxes, bound with metal straps and bearing handwritten identification codes. Initially one of the robbers marched up to the cartons in the corner and snapped off one of the lids.

Inside the first box opened were 12 perfectly formed bars of pure gold. As if to check the robbers weren't dreaming, a few more lids were prized off to reveal the same awesome sight.

For a few moments, the gang stood and stared at the gold in stunned silence. They couldn't quite believe their eyes. How could so much gold be held in one place at a single moment? It was more than the gang could ever have imagined. Then, the robbers snapped out of their daze and began hurriedly passing bars between themselves to their battered Ford

Transit, which was parked in the loading bay of the warehouse. Within minutes their unexpected windfall was starting to make the vehicle's axles bend with the weight. More than one eyewitness later reported seeing an old van with a wheezing engine riding very low on its suspension through the streets of nearby Hounslow some minutes after the robbery.

Inside those 60 grey boxes were 6,800 gold bars, weighing a total of three-and-a-half tons and worth £26,369,778. Also in the vault at Unit 7 were several hundred thousand pounds in used bank notes locked in three safes. One pouch contained traveller's cheques worth £200,000. In the other were polished and rough diamonds valued at £113,000.

Box after box was opened and a veritable Aladdin's cave of treasure was revealed. The atmosphere ramped up as, with scarcely concealed excitement, the gang frantically moved the gold and money into their waiting van. No one within the robbers' immediate circle had any experience of dealing with this amount of gold – the gang had only been expecting to find cash – so they were already thinking about who they would need to call in for help to disperse the gold.

As that rusting old Transit van scraped its way out of the warehouse, none of those robbers could have known they were in possession of something so dangerous that it would eventually cost many of them and their associates their lives. The lives of a lot of people – both innocent and not so innocent – were about to be blighted forever.

Scotland Yard Commander Frank Cater, 56, needed the Brink's-Mat job like he needed the proverbial hole in the head.

Months before the raid, another "firm" of London robbers had coolly taken £6 million in used banknotes during that Easter 1983 raid on a Security Express depot on the edge of the City of London. On that occasion, a guard had also been doused in petrol.

That job had been dubbed the "Crime of the Decade" by the tabloids. Cater wondered if the same gang was now also responsible for the Brink's-Mat raid, which would quickly earn an even more dramatic title: "The Crime of the Century." After all, before these two raids, the previous holder of the title had been the Great Train Robbery back in 1963, and that had netted a relatively paltry sum compared to this one.

One of the first senior detectives to arrive at the scene immediately described the raid as a "typical Old Kent Road armed robbery", executed with customary efficiency and ruthlessness. The police knew perfectly well in which corner of London they should concentrate their inquiries, but breaking down the barriers that existed between the law and the gangsters in that part of the city was another thing altogether.

Less than 48 hours after the Brink's-Mat robbery, Lloyd's of London announced a reward of £2 million for information leading to the return of the Brink's-Mat gold, which had already leapt in value by more than £20 an ounce since the robbery had taken place.

Rather than disappear in the days following the robbery, McAvoy and Robinson told the other gang members to make sure they hung around their usual haunts, because if they disappeared it would be sure to alert the police to their involvement. Not surprisingly, as word spread across the underworld about the magnitude of the job and the vast amount of gold that had been stolen, various top London faces let it be known that they would be pitching for the "rights" to turn all that gold into ready cash.

McAvoy and Robinson steadfastly refused to deal with any such criminals initially because they didn't want to give the law any excuse to pull them in. They believed they'd get away with their audacious crime if they kept cool and low-key, but there was one obvious, glaring weakness on the horizon – Robinson's brother-in-law Tony Black. He wasn't a villain and Black was, in the words of one robber, "bricking himself". Robinson got a message to Black telling him not to worry and that the police would probably pull him in as an obvious inside man, but as long as he said nothing they would never get any proof of his involvement.

McAvoy, Robinson and the rest of the gang split up after a quick meeting at a south London flophouse following the raid. They were all under strict instructions not to communicate with each other for at least a month. Usually at flophouses the proceeds of a robbery are split between the gang members, but on this occasion the team all agreed that they would have to sit on the gold for some time before starting to turn it into hard cash.

Not all of the robbers were happy about this "arrangement", but McAvoy and Robinson made it clear there was no choice in the matter. However, the sheer size of the gold bullion was only the start of their problems. McAvoy later told one associate that all the gang members knew only too well that the police would be put under enormous pressure to solve the robbery because of the vast amount of gold that had been stolen. The gang had effectively single-handedly "humiliated" Scotland Yard.

And, of course, of the six Brink's-Mat guards on duty that morning, Tony Black stuck out like Ronnie Kray at a Boy Scouts' meeting. The fact that Black had been out of sight of the others in the minutes before the raid was also significant. Within hours of the raid being carried out, the police began to put together some damning intelligence on Black. Principally that his brother-in-law, Brian Robinson, was a renowned blagger on the south London criminal circuit.

The police knew all about Brian Robinson. Over the previous two years, he'd escaped prosecution for two armed robbery charges. A magistrate threw out one of the cases because of insufficient evidence; the other, for handling money taken in an armed raid, was dropped when the Director of Public Prosecutions (DPP) decided there was not enough evidence to bring about a conviction.

Despite the obvious link between the two men, the police decided to bide their time when it came to Tony Black and they held back from arresting him. Instead, they put a shadow on him in the hope he might lead detectives to the actual robbers. It looked as if McAvoy and Robinson's strict instructions to the whole team that none of the blaggers should see each other amounted to good advice. The same applied to any further contact with the "wobbly" Tony Black – the biggest weak link of the entire Brink's-Mat job. For virtually a week, Black was shadowed by police and was seen making numerous, nervous-looking calls from phone boxes. However, it seemed that he never actually got to talk to who-ever it was he was calling, because he'd end up slamming the phone down and cursing as he left phone box after phone box.

Black and the other guards were eventually called back to the Brink's-Mat warehouse to help police make a reconstruction video of what exactly had happened. Afterwards, police were struck by how nervous Black looked throughout the reconstruction, although they knew that alone wasn't enough evidence to arrest him. They needed a confession and they were sure that would come with time. The "let-him-stew" philosophy was a tried and trusted police technique and it looked sure to work this time as well. The police were convinced that if they bided their time, Tony Black would eventually crumble.

At 8am on Sunday, 4 December – just eight days after the Brink's-Mat robbery – all six guards on duty on the day of the robbery were taken to Hounslow Police Station for questioning. It was all a charade: only Tony Black was properly interrogated. He was questioned and re-questioned about his movements on the day of the robbery and subsequently for six hours. Eventually, Scotland Yard investigator Detective Inspector Tony Brightwell rose to his feet and told Black: 'There are certain points which have arisen as a result of the original statement which you made, the video reconstruction of events and during this interview… to put it bluntly, we are not happy with your story. We will leave you to have a re-think."

The detective and his colleague then left the interview room and – using yet another tried and trusted police manual technique – let him sweat for more than an hour while they discussed his story over coffee in the canteen.

Brightwell and his colleague returned to the interview room at 4.52pm. They were certain of their ground, and the investigators planned to execute what they hoped would be their coup de grace.

They then deliberately took their time taking down Black's statement all over again, going through every detail with him – in order to rack up the tension. It wasn't until the early hours of the following day, 5 December 1983, that a detective sergeant accompanied by two colleagues completed Black's 21-page statement after more than eight hours of questioning. To put it simply, they wore Tony Black down and down until he told them about his involvement.

Afterwards, Black admitted to investigators: "I'm feeling much better now. It's like a weight off my mind. It was just too big. I couldn't handle it. There's one thing, though. I'm worried about these people, what they're going to do to me…"

Minutes later, Commander Frank Cater entered the room and waved his three detectives out. They believed they already knew the identity of one of Robinson's accomplices. Black said that he thought the surname of the big man known as "Tony" was a notorious south London blagger called Tony White. Criminal intelligence had already confirmed that Tony White and another criminal, Mickey McAvoy, were known acquaintances of Robinson. It was also known that White owned a vehicle similar to a car seen circling the trading estate a few days before the robbery.

The three detectives, who'd left the interview room, went straight downstairs to collect the mug shots they'd already put to one side from police files. There were two folders, each containing 12 photographs of various individuals. They placed mug shots of McAvoy and White in each batch.

Shortly before midnight, after Commander Cater had finished with Black, DS Branch pushed the carefully collated folders under Black's nose. The first file was opened and the pictures were spread across the table. Black immediately pointed to a photo of Mickey McAvoy.

"That's Mick," he said. He had confirmed the detectives' suspicions. The photograph he pointed to was of the man the other guards had dubbed "The Bully", aka "Mad Micky McAvoy".

They pushed the second folder across the table and Black again picked out another photo almost immediately. "That's Tony," he declared. It was a photograph of Tony White.

In the early hours of Tuesday, 6 December, Tony Black was led back to his cell, understandably wondering if he had just sentenced himself to death. The gang might still be out and about enjoying their liberty, but, thanks to Black, detectives knew it was only a matter of time before they'd have them under lock and key.

Black was not a professional criminal. Having made a full, detailed, precise confession, Black then agreed with detectives to turn Queen's evidence. Of the original five-man gang, he had fingered three of them: Brian Robinson, Mickey McAvoy and Tony White.

But, for the time being, detectives decided to continue playing a waiting game. They suspected that once the trio knew that Black had grassed on them then they'd probably try and make a run for it. Before they did so, they were hoping the villains might first lead them to the gold. It was a risky strategy, but the sheer size of the raid meant that none of the usual rules applied.

Then, a month after the robbery, Flying Squad officer Bill Miller got a tip-off that a man had been seen in London's Hatton Garden jewellery district trying to buy an industrial gold smelter. A week later, Miller was undercover in Worcestershire, watching the smelter being loaded into the back of a gold Rolls Royce. "He was easy to follow because the smelter was too big for the Rolls and the boot wouldn't close," explained Miller. "So we followed him all the way back to Kent." The car was parked up outside a cottage while the driver went inside.

Miller stayed with the vehicle all night and was relieved by a specialist surveillance team in the morning. When the driver returned to the car, the team followed on behind. "Within five minutes they lost him," Miller later recalled. When they returned to the cottage later in the day the smelter had gone.

The driver of that Rolls Royce was a man called Mickey Lawson, 35, who happened to be best friends with Kenneth Noye, 36, who would emerge as one of the key figures involved in handling of the Brink's-Mat gold bullion. Lawson had actually purchased the smelter from William Allday and Co. Ltd in Stourport-on-Severn. The Rolls Royce was soon regularly seen at Noye's house in Kent. One of Lawson's fingerprints would eventually be found inside that same house. The operating instructions for the smelter they had seen in the back of that Rolls Royce were also found in Kenneth Noye's shed.

AFTERMATH

Police believed at least 15 people were involved the Brink's-Mat robbery and the operation to launder the gold bullion, but only three of the gang members were ever convicted. Mickey McAvoy and Brian Robinson were both jailed for 25 years in December 1984, and Kenneth Noye served 14 years for VAT fraud connected to handling some of the stolen gold. Noye was released in 1990, but ten years later was convicted of murdering Stephen Cameron in a road-rage fight on the M25 and is now serving a life sentence.

In the 30 years since the Brink's-Mat robbery was committed there have been many changes in the underworld, but one common denominator still links the old with the new – the tens of millons of pounds worth of Brink's-Mat gold that remains missing and which has sparked a long and deadly battle between rival villains.

In 2000, detectives searching for the missing gold were tipped off about a "burial site" on the south coast of England. Officers used hi-tech imaging equipment to search a timber yard behind a builders' merchants in Graystone Lane, off Old London Road, Hastings, in East Sussex. After initially conducting virtually a fingertip search, a pneumatic drill was then used to dig deeper in the covered yard. A Scotland Yard spokeswoman told reporters at the scene: "This search is based on information we have received following a lengthy inquiry which has lasted many months. I cannot say exactly what we are looking for. A drill has been used to dig into the concrete floor of the yard."

But nothing was ever found and there was a deep

suspicion that the original "tip" was given to Brink's-Mat detectives simply in order to divert them away from other more "relevant" areas. Cat-and-mouse games had been played ever since the robbery and they showed no signs of stopping.

In 2005, Scotland Yard detectives found six suitcases crammed with gold inside a London deposit box. Not surprisingly, they suspected that the gold might be connected to the Brink's-Mat robbery. The gold "grains" were carefully wrapped in plastic and wedged inside travel luggage. They'd been found after police raided a deposit box as part of their ongoing Brink's-Mat investigation.

Commander Allan Gibson of Scotland Yard's specialist crime directorate told reporters his officers had never seen anything like it. He even admitted the suitcases were so heavy that his officers struggled to pick them up. The haul was said to be the single largest discovery of unexplained gold ever found in Britain. Provisional estimates suggested the suitcases' contents could be worth £8 million. Alongside the gold, Scotland Yard officers also found £30 million in cash, much of it stuffed into plastic supermarket bags, which police believed were also the profits of organized crime, but they have never managed to prove that it came from the Brink's-Mat robbery.

But the highly publicized discovery also brought back to the public eye the fact that it was still very unclear how much – if any – of the Brink's-Mat bullion had ever actually been recovered.

The police continued to face ever-mounting criticism about their sometimes-clumsy attempts to find the remaining gold.

Insurance investigator Bob McCann explained in 2001: "It's an open secret 'Mad Mickey' McAvoy went straight under police surveillance (after his release from prison) in the hope he'd lead them to the gold, but so far he's just led them on a merry little dance. These characters are not stupid. They knew they were being watched."

And then there are the numerous other incidents, irrefutably linked to the biggest robbery of the last century. In late 1997, Brink's-Mat cash helped finance an audacious plot to spring a major villain from inside a British jail. The extraordinary escape plan involved smuggling in quantities of Semtex explosive, blasting a hole in the jail wall and flying the villain to freedom by helicopter. One employee at top security Whitemoor Prison, in Cambridgeshire, was arrested after an inmate leaked the escape plans to prison authorities. The gang was planning to "spring" one of Brink's-Mat gold-bullion handler Kenneth Noye's oldest criminal associates, south Londoner George Caccavale, 56. He was serving 18 years inside Whitemoor for his part as the leader of a nine-man gang that was jailed for a total of 167 years at Bristol Crown Court in July 1997 for their part in a £65 million drug-smuggling operation.

Certain members of the Brink's-Mat gang, besides Noye, decided to help finance the escape bid because Caccavale had been a loyal and trusted associate to the team, even after he was arrested. But even more importantly, some of the robbers had also invested millions of pounds in Caccavale's drugs operation and wanted a "return" on their money. It's a measure of the power these Brink's-Mat villains believed they held that they would even consider such an audacious plan.

So, in November 1997, three Brink's-Mat associates travelled by private jet to Spain's Costa del Sol to meet a gang of well-known drug dealers and armed robbers who'd agreed to acquire the Semtex and hire a helicopter for the prison-escape plan. The gang even had an informant working inside Whitemoor, who was prepared to smuggle the Semtex into the prison. This employee had been trapped into helping the gang because he'd been caught in a compromising position with a woman who had been planted by the criminals. The same man was also smuggling drugs into Whitemoor for some of the inmates.

Following an anonymous tip-off, prison authorities foiled the escape plan just a week before it was due to be carried out. They'd become particularly sensitive to such problems since the 1994 escape of six inmates, including five IRA terrorists, from the same jail.

It later emerged that the Brink's-Mat gang were furious that the jail-break plan had been foiled because they lost a fortune in Caccavale's drugs business as well as spending hundreds of thousands of pounds on the escape preparations. "We're talking about paying informants, safe houses, new vehicles, private planes. None of it comes cheap," explained one who should know.

Around the same time, Kenneth Noye – on the run after killing a motorist on the M25 – used Brink's-Mat cash to buy a £200,000 yacht in Cadiz, Spain, and immediately sub-leased it out to rival hashish gangs to use for drug smuggling from Morocco. Noye also invested half a million pounds of Brink's-Mat money in a carefully planned hashish-smuggling operation through one of the most notorious criminals in Gibraltar – just a two-hour drive from Noye's Spanish hideaway south of Cadiz. Noye entered the British colony on foot using a false UK passport and his picture ID wasn't checked by border patrol officers from either Spain or Britain.

Many of the Brink's-Mat gang and their closest associates in the drugs trade were not having such an easy time, though. So-called heroin king James Hamill was jailed for 18 years in February 1998 after being found guilty of running one of Britain's fastest-growing heroin supply rings. The police believe that some of the Brink's-Mat proceeds were "invested" in Hamill's operation. Hamill, 38, had aspirations to become one of Europe's most powerful godfathers and he'd taken a lot of advice from two particular members of the Brink's-Mat gang over the years. They'd encouraged Hamill to steer clear of using any drugs himself – a rule that, ironically, most of them broke with regularity when it came to cocaine, although none of them would ever touch heroin.

Kenneth Noye himself wasn't recaptured until the summer of 1998 when British and Spanish detectives swooped on him as he was eating dinner with his mistress at a restaurant in the quiet fishing town of Barbate, a few miles north of his secret hideaway home on a rock overlooking the Atlantic Ocean.

Many believe to this day that Noye may well have been tracked down after certain other members of the Brink's-Mat gang decided to "sing" to the police because they were fed up with all the unwelcome public attention Noye had been getting, especially since his involvement in the road-rage killing of Stephen Cameron on the M25.

Then, shortly after Noye's arrest in Spain for the killing, there was a rare sighting of a notorious villain who had tried to keep his connections to the Brink's-Mat job secret. That character was Mickey "The Pimpernel" Green, a classic London armed robber of the 1970s and '80s whose role in the Brink's-Mat heist has never been revealed before. Suffice to say, he's known as "The Pimpernel" because of his ability to avoid arrest. Many inside the police remain convinced to this day that Green is one of the Brink's-Mat gang never bought to justice and they call him "The One Who Got Away".

Green first became involved with the Brink's-Mat crew after teaming up with an old robber associate and developing a lucrative VAT scam on gold krugerrands. They bought the gold coins – which didn't carry VAT – then melted them down into ingots and sold them back to the bullion house, collecting a hefty wedge of VAT in the process. It was reckoned Green and his pals made £6 million in under a year.

As a result, Green was brought in ahead of the Brink's-Mat job as a "consultant". But then, some believe, Green convinced the gang's leader, "Mad Mickey" McAvoy, to let him join the actual team of blaggers. After the job, Green then helped the gang set up their own VAT-avoidance scam, which is believed to have added at least £10 million to the profits from the heist gold itself.

Within two years of the Brink's-Mat raid, Green – described by UK and Eire lawmakers as one of the world's biggest cocaine traffickers – was released on a legal technicality in Spain after having been arrested on suspicion of drugs smuggling. Since Brink's-Mat, Green had become the classic Mister Big with alleged links to the Mafia and Colombian drug cartels. He was a regular visitor to South America, where he nailed down a number of huge cocaine deals with the world-famous drug baron, Pablo Escobar, who was later killed by drug enforcement agents in 1993.

Certain members of the Brink's-Mat gang entrusted Green with a lot cash because they knew the vast profits that could be made from cocaine if it was purchased direct from the "source" in Colombia. Spending money on drug deals was also a great way to launder the proceeds from the gold. Green wasn't in the slightest bit fazed by travelling to places like Medellin, in Colombia – a city that was virtually ruled by the drug cartels.

Over the years, British, Dutch, French and US authorities, all of who suspected him of major criminal activities, had shadowed Green. There had even been a rumour that he kept £1 million in French francs hidden in a box buried under a flowerbed at his Marbella villa.

When American DEA agents monitoring many of the big Colombian drug barons reported that a "limey" criminal had been in a series of meetings with gangsters, they passed on his name and details to their colleagues at Scotland Yard, but there was nothing anyone could do without any more concrete evidence. Detectives in London also reckoned that Green should be allowed to continue setting up cocaine deals in the hope that he might eventually lead them to the rest of the Brink's-Mat gold.

Green always returned from his trips to Medellin looking as if he didn't have a care in the world. He believed he was untouchable in Spain at that time. His grand-looking hacienda, just east of Marbella, was worth more than £2 million and he'd even got a friend to live in a gatehouse to keep an eye on the property whenever he was on his travels.

Then Green was yet again arrested by Spanish police after two tons of hash was seized, but he mysteriously got bail and fled to Morocco, leaving behind 11 powerboats and yachts allegedly used to run drugs from North Africa to Spain. Green eventually turned up in Paris. Interpol was alerted and French police swooped on his swish Left Bank apartment where they found gold bullion and cocaine, but no Mickey Green.

That gold was allegedly part of the Brink's-Mat consignment and it backed up suspicions that he was using the gold to buy shipments of cocaine directly from the Colombian cartels. Green was later sentenced to 17 years in jail in his absence for possessing the drugs and for smuggling. Green's next stop was California, where he rented Rod Stewart's mansion under an alias. A few months later, FBI agents knocked his front door down as he was lounging by the pool and arrested him. Green was put on a flight bound for France to serve that 17-year jail sentence, but got off when the plane made a stopover at Ireland's Shannon Airport. Using his Irish passport, he slipped unnoticed past customs men and headed for Dublin where he had many contacts. Green then took full advantage of the weak extradition laws between Eire and France at the time and settled in Dublin.

He even splashed out on a massive half-million-pound farmhouse just outside the city. But Green then ran a red light at a busy junction in his Bentley and killed a local taxi driver called Joe White. He was fined and banned from driving, but there was uproar in the local press because he was not given a custodial sentence, despite the death of an innocent man. Under mounting pressure, Eire police made it clear they were planning to grab Green's assets, including the farmhouse, so the Londoner disappeared yet again. During another criminal's trial in London, it was later claimed that Green bribed two witnesses in the death-crash court case to keep him out of jail. Shortly after leaving Eire, Green turned up once again in Spain and simply carried on where he had left off, still apparently untouchable on the Costa del Crime.

Today Mickey Green is rumoured to spend much of his time in Costa Rica, where he owns yet another luxury home. He's also alleged to have links to property in Thailand.

But characters like Mickey Green really got up the nose of Brink's-Mat robbery top dog "Mad Mickey" McAvoy, because he suspected Green and others were spending his share of the Brink's-Mat gold, even though McAvoy made it crystal clear over and over again that he was fully expecting to be given all "his" gold when he was released from prison after serving his sentence.

McAvoy and co-robber Brian Robinson had also been following Kenneth Noye's exploits especially closely from their prison cells. Not only did Noye's continual hogging of the newspaper headlines cause them more "aggro" with the police, but it also grated with them that Noye was now the best known of all the so-called Brink's-Mat gang – and he hadn't even been directly involved in the robbery itself.

Both men were careful to keep a clean sheet inside Leicester's Long Lartin prison, because they were patiently biding their time in the expectation that many millions of pounds awaited them on their release. Even when other inmates at the prison attempted a mass breakout, the two Brink's-Mat kingpins kept a low profile and refused to budge. Thirty prisoners had barricaded themselves on a landing after guards foiled their escape bid. As a consequence of this and other security breeches, the prison was upgraded to a maximum-security prison, but staff noted that McAvoy and Robinson had played absolutely no role in the trouble.

In late 2000, McAvoy was finally released (Robinson was released some months later and disappeared into thin air) after serving almost 20 years for the heist and he slipped out of prison virtually unnoticed around the same time as Kenneth Noye was being sentencing for that M25 road-rage killing.

Behind the scenes, McAvoy put out "the word" to all "relevant parties" that he was expecting his share of the gold to be delivered to him at the right moment. The responses he started to get back made it clear that it was not going to be handed to him on a plate. That's when McAvoy decided it was time to flex his muscles. If the gold wasn't going to be brought to him, then he'd go looking for it himself. And God help anyone who got in his way.

McAvoy lived on the borders between south-east London and Kent, the so-called "Garden of England", where criminality thrives to this very day. The power and influence of the Brink's-Mat gang and a number of other legendary faces made Kent the perfect gateway to the lucrative drugs markets of Europe. One retired bank robber even made a small fortune running an unofficial "ferry service" from a tiny port near Dover across to Holland, where drug barons would then travel to "company meetings" in Amsterdam before slipping back into Kent unnoticed.

"You could get in and out of Europe without the cozzers (the police) knowing anything about your movements," recalled bank robber Gordon Scott. "The fella who ran it had this tasty motor launch complete with bedrooms, a fully stocked bar and he'd even bring on the dancing girls if you booked well in advance."

The area of Kent countryside stretching from Kenneth Noye's one-time hometown of West Kingsdown past Biggin Hill – and its handy airstrip – and across to Swanley was known to Brink's-Mat detectives as "The Bermuda Triangle". As one senior police officer explained: "Things went in there and had a habit of never coming out again. And we're talking about everything from people to lorry-loads of bootlegged fags 'n' booze, not to mention gold." The construction of the nearby M25 ensured easy access to the Bermuda Triangle at all times of the day and night.

There have been almost two dozen killings with direct connections to the Brink's-Mat robbery and its team of blaggers. Those killings included the death of 63-year-old Brink's-Mat robber Brian Perry, who was shot down in broad daylight in 2001 as he got out of his car in Bermondsey, south-east London. That "commission" sent a shiver of fear throughout the underworld. A masked hitman, dressed in dark clothes, aimed and fired at Perry's head, chest and back. Perry was found lying in a pool of his own blood after local residents heard the gunshots. The masked assassin escaped in a dark car fitted with false number plates. It sped off towards the Old Kent Road shortly after the shooting. Perry had been murdered in cold blood, right in the heart of his "home territory".

Whoever commissioned the hit was sending out a very clear "message".

Detectives and gangsters alike believed Perry's death was yet more evidence of the deadly ongoing feud between certain members of the Brink's-Mat gang. Naturally, it sent out a terrifying message to other villains. One source very close to many of the gang, told this author: "Certain people wanted their share of the gold and when it wasn't there waiting for them they started getting very upset."

Latest victim Perry had earlier served a nine-year prison sentence for his role in laundering profits from the Brink's-Mat raid. At the time of his murder, it was strongly rumoured that Perry knew where at least £10 million worth of the gold from the heist remained hidden. One source also claimed that Perry was suspected of secretly helping the police with their inquiries and that may have been the "last straw" as far as his enemies were concerned. "A lot of people were saying that Perry was 'helping' the cozzers," said one Brink's-Mat associate. "He signed his own death warrant if that really was the case."

And so the cycle of Brink's-Mat death and destruction continued. A few months after Perry's death, two of his oldest associates were murdered near the busy Kent ports of Chatham and Rochester. Jon Bristow, 39, and Ray Chapman, 44, had both bought boats shortly before they were killed separately. In the south-east London underworld it was said that the men had been "bigging it up" with wads of Brink's-Mat cash they said Perry had given them for "services rendered".

In November 2001, the trial of the two men accused of killing Brian Perry was abandoned when both men were acquitted after the prosecution admitted the only evidence available was circumstantial.

To this day detectives believe that other villains are trying to make sure Kenneth Noye never gets released from jail by deliberately killing some of his known enemies to make it look as if the murders have been "commissioned" by Noye. As one south London underworld source explained: "Think about it... it does make sense... It would explain why the execution was carried out in such a public manner. Also, a lot of 'chaps' had the incentive to frame Noye."

Meanwhile the fallouts between the Brink's-Mat gang continued. There were strong rumours that Noye was feuding from inside jail with his fellow gold "expert" John "Goldfinger" Palmer, who'd lent Noye his private jet three years earlier so he could leave the country following the M25 murder. Sources in the London underworld said Noye and Palmer were at "daggers with each other" and as a result both men were carefully kept in separate prisons "for their own safety". Noye was being kept under round-the-clock guard in top security Whitemoor Prison, in Cambridgeshire, while Palmer remained at an undisclosed jail.

In south-east London, some less important faces with links to the Brink's-Mat robbery were having problems of a different nature. Take Clifford Norris, who also happened to be the father of one of the youths accused of the racist killing of a black student called Stephen Lawrence at a bus-stop in south London back in 1991. A slim, almost fragile man of no more than 5 feet 7 inches, Norris had at one time used Brink's-Mat money to help finance a drug-importation business.

When his son John was arrested for the murder of Stephen Lawrence, Clifford Norris immediately tried to use his Brink's-Mat contacts to put pressure on the police to release his son. Links between the Brink's-Mat gang and the Norris family seem to support these claims, which prove even further that the robbery influenced a vast range of events. Clifford Norris was eventually arrested and sentenced to nine-and-a-half years for drugs and firearm offences.

And still the Brink's-Mat killings continued. On 14 May 2003, Brink's-Mat gang member George Francis, now in his sixties, was gunned down at point-blank range as he sat in his car outside the courier business he ran in south-east London. He should have known better after being injured by another shooter 17 years earlier, but "Georgie Boy" reckoned he was untouchable.

Brink's-Mat insurance investigator Bob McCann – who'd spent years tracking the missing gold – later said he believed both Francis and Perry were probably "quite literally fishing for gold and they got too close" and paid for it with their lives.

Murder squad detectives immediately sought out Mickey McAvoy to ask him about Francis's execution, but there was no evidence linking McAvoy to any of the Brink's-Mat murders committed since his release from prison. Despite having no obvious job, McAvoy seemed to have a comfortable lifestyle. As well as his luxury home in Kent, he also often flew to Spain's Costa del Sol, where he had access to a beachside hacienda

Meanwhile Brink's-Mat's tentacles continued to spread far and wide. The previously unfashionable Mediterranean island territory of northern Cyprus was transformed into an even more dangerous version of the Costa del Crime thanks to a handful of Brink's-Mat associated villains. Money from the heist helped set up timeshare resorts, build hotels and enable a number of gangsters with links to the robbery to buy large detached mansions on the island.

On a five-mile stretch of the coast between the port of Kyrenia and the town of Lapta, Brink's-Mat faces openly lived a champagne lifestyle in luxury homes. Less than a mile from the centre of the northern Cyprus town of Lapta was the secluded £2 million villa of Dogan Arif, the unofficial leader of the Arifs gangland family, who terrorized south London with their robbing and drug trafficking operations in the 1980s and who also played a role in handling much of the Brink's-Mat gold.

One of the most notorious of the regular visitors to northern Cyprus was Brian Wright, the so-called "Milkman" who'd also been involved in laundering Brink's-Mat proceeds for a number of years. Wright had even used some Brink's-Mat cash to partly finance a gang that flooded Britain with £500 million worth of cocaine back in 1999–2000. By all accounts, Wright enjoyed a lavish lifestyle in northern Cyprus until the long arm of the law eventually caught up with him.

And still the murderous links to Brink's-Mat kept coming thick and fast. In 2008, a bodybuilder claimed in court he dismembered a number of possible Brink's-Mat victims on behalf of north London criminal family, the Adams Family. "A Team" chief Terry Adams, was believed to have made a fortune laundering some of the Brink's-Mat gold. Potential witnesses had been too terrified to testify against Terry

Adams but he was eventually jailed in 2007 for seven years for the relatively minor charge of money laundering.

As one senior detective who worked on and off on the Brink's-Mat investigation for more than 20 years commented: "Nothing really surprises us any more when it comes to Brink's-Mat. These villains were out of control. Many of them were off their heads on drugs bought with their newfound riches. The trouble was that when that money either ran out, or in the case of some of them never materialized, there was only one way to respond and that was to kill people to show others that even many years after the robbery was committed, if they dared to cross the gang they would still pay for it with their life."

And so it is that the Brink's-Mat heist continues to overshadow the lives of so many people.

6. WHAT GOES AROUND, COMES AROUND

"I was as addicted to robbery as I was to cocaine. The rush from pulling off a job was better than anything in the world, including sex."

Valerio Viccei

Teramo, Italy, April 2000

The veteran detective walked reluctantly into the ice-cold morgue in the basement of the local hospital to inspect the bullet-riddled corpse of the man killed in a shootout with police earlier that day. He forced himself to look down at the body because he had to be sure it really was him. The corpse's hair was flecked with grey, dressed in blue jeans and a green jacket, body punctured by a hail of machine-gun bullets, blots of dried blood seeping from his eyes, nose and mouth.

The detective took a deep breath and stood silently over the body. His eyes scanned what remained of the face to the bloodied, twisted upper torso. He felt a mixture of pain and anger, a sense of relief and also of dread. He felt relief because the nightmare of life was finally over for this evil man, which meant there would be no more innocent victims. Dread because the detective feared this killing might unleash yet more violence. It was time it ended. Enough is enough, he thought to himself. Let all the pain and bloodshed die with him.

After a lifetime of committing crimes, one of the world's most notorious villains was back home in Italy in his final resting place. The detective nodded to the morgue assistant and then supplied him with the information to be written on a small card tag which was then tied around the victim's toe: *"Valerio Viccei, cause of death, gunshot wounds"*

Just 13 years earlier, he'd been the king of the London underworld.

Knightsbridge, London, 12 July 1987

Knightsbridge, a stone's throw from Buckingham Palace, in the heart of London. The rich and famous dominate this part of the capital. Well, they did, until Valerio Viccei decided to pull off one of the biggest robberies in criminal history. Viccei was a playboy with a taste for guns, cocaine and women who were as fast as his wheels.

The son of a lawyer, Viccei, aged 31, had arrived in London the previous year from Italy, where he was wanted for

50 armed robberies. Within weeks, he'd obtained a Beretta semi-automatic pistol and started holding up banks in Britain's capital city.

Viccei decided to stash his loot and gun in a place called the Knightsbridge Safe Deposit Centre. Then he discovered the owner, Parvez Latif, had a weakness for cocaine and that his business was losing money. Viccei moved in on Latif – and even began a secret affair with Latif's girlfriend Pamela Seamarks.

Viccei later claimed he told Latif that if he had the right insurance, a robbery at the Knightsbridge Centre was the best thing that could happen to him. Latif was so broke at the time he didn't take a lot of persuading. And when Viccei heard about the riches rumoured to be hidden at the safe deposit centre opposite luxury store Harrods, he decided it would be his next target. Viccei, the professional robber saw this one as the job that would set him up for life, although even he had no idea just how big a haul he would scoop.

Viccei had come to London in search of new opportunities and now he reckoned he'd found his own yellow-brick road. He later admitted: "I had a passion for weapons, beautiful women and fast cars." It was all coming together perfectly for the master criminal showman.

On the day of the robbery, Viccei and his accomplice, Eric Rubin, 47, entered the Knightsbridge Safe Deposit Centre and requested to rent a safe deposit box. After being shown into the vault, they produced handguns and subdued the duty manager and security guards.

The two men then hung a sign on the street-level door explaining that the Safe Deposit Centre was temporarily closed, while letting in further robbers. Viccei threatened one worker in the vault: "Don't move. Don't even breath, or you will regret it, pal. Now, get down on the floor very slowly and keep your hands above your head. Good, that's a good man. Put them behind your back. That's fine."

Then Viccei told his partner: "Jack, if the punk makes a move, just blow his legs off right away and he won't bother us any more."

Viccei later claimed he didn't mean it, but many believe he would have shot the man without hesitation if he had not done as he was told.

Security guard uniforms, metal cutting equipment, walkie-talkies and the owner's complicity ultimately enabled Viccei's gang to clear 114 boxes over a weekend inside the safe deposit centre. The victims included royalty, celebrities, millionaires and criminals. No shots were fired and no one was injured. As Viccei later told the world: "It was the perfect fucking job."

One hour after the robbers departed Knightsbridge, the shift changed and the new staff discovered the crime and alerted the police. It was one of the simplest and – in criminal terms – smoothest robberies ever committed. Cold, calculating and carefully timed. Police had no doubt they were dealing with a very experienced team of blaggers.

The haul was so vast that Viccei filled his bath with banknotes and covered the floor of his flat in Hampstead, north London, with glittering jewels. One diamond alone was worth over £4 million.

Viccei later explained: "The money was much more than I had expected it to be. It was all in large denomination bills, neatly packed and in so many different currencies that some of them were totally alien to me.

"Everything was so out of proportion that I needed to think carefully about my next moves, but in the end I decided I could not afford to think at all.

"The carpet of my bedroom floor was entirely covered by a sea of diamonds, rubies, emeralds, sapphires, pearls, gold... and every other sort of treasure you could think of. There was so much of it that it would be impossible to walk around without wearing slippers.

"One single diamond was 41 carats, many others were well over 20. Some of the necklaces, with stones the size of a one-pound coin, had hundreds of other diamonds on them and the sun seemed to be specially attracted by this unique display of nature's pride.

"I didn't want to miss a single second of it. I walked back to the bed and sat down on it, my head resting on a pyramid of pillows. In the middle of the room was a Persian carpet and on this I had piled all the cash; its amount was staggering beyond belief.

"I didn't have time to count all of it, but from what I already knew, it came to millions. Next to me sat a gold tray on which I had placed a rock of pure cocaine weighing over a kilo (he'd found it in one of the boxes). I reached for the golden tray and snipped a fragment off the huge rock of cocaine. I grabbed a platinum credit card belonging to some asshole with three family names and five titles just to cut myself a line of this beautiful stuff. Then I rolled a 1,000 Swiss franc bank note and zapped it in one go! I lay on my back again and took a long breath of pride and satisfaction. I rested my hands behind my head and said very quietly, 'I did it!'"

The true value of Viccei's haul was never known as more than 30 keyholders failed to come forward following the robbery. In some ways that made it an even more perfect crime, because the police would never know exactly what had been stolen. Once again, Viccei's luck seemed to be with him. Today it is estimated that his haul was worth £40 million (equivalent to £140 million today). But even professionals like Valerio Viccei make mistakes…

Three days later, police forensic officers found a bloody fingerprint on one of the boxes where Viccei had cut himself breaking the lock. Detectives eventually found it was a match to a set the Italian authorities had sent over a few weeks before in their quest to trace wanted bank robber Valerio Viccei. By mid-August 1987, several of Viccei's London accomplices were under Flying Squad surveillance, but detectives believed that Viccei himself had fled to Latin America.

A few weeks later, one of the other robbery suspects, Agostino Vallorani, was twice seen driving past White's Hotel in Bayswater Road looking at a black Ferrari. Then officers found that the owner of the vehicle, Israel Pinkas, had been given a parking ticket outside the hotel.

A surveillance team followed Pinkas and, a short while later, Valerio Viccei turned up at White's, which was renowned as his favourite hotel in the world. Detectives watched as Viccei parked up his own £100,000 red Ferrari sports car. A few minutes later, he emerged from the hotel and drove off in the direction of Marble Arch. It caught the detectives by surprise: they hadn't expected Viccei to spend so little time in the hotel.

So Flying Squad Detective Inspector Dick Leach and his team moved off behind Viccei's Ferrari. Leach knew he could easily lose Viccei in the dense traffic, so he took a risky decision to swoop on the Italian as soon as possible. A couple of minutes later, five unmarked police cars boxed in Viccei in a dramatic stop-and-search operation at Marble Arch. The road was stopped in both directions as armed detectives leapt onto the bonnet of Viccei's Ferrari, smashed a hole in the front windscreen and literally dragged Viccei out. Typically, Viccei later claimed that he'd been caught in much more dramatic fashion after trying to escape by screeching off in his sports car. In reality, however, he came relatively quietly. Police found £2 million of valuables stolen from the Knightsbridge vaults in the boot of his Ferrari.

Viccei's own "top spin" on how he was arrested is worth reading, because it proves just how much of showman he really was: "I immediately realized that my chances of escape were nonexistent, but I had a go. As I accelerated, the Ferrari's large tyres squeaked on the asphalt, but I had nowhere to go. The game was up and I knew it. My windscreen was smashed and I was literally dragged through it. Any resistance would have been pointless and almost comical. Half a dozen cops were trying to handcuff me at once and not being very kind to me either – not one little bit!"

Police recorded Viccei as saying the following words after his capture: "Right, chaps, the game is up now and you have no need to be nasty. You are the winners so calm down and everything is going to be fine!"

Later in court, Viccei proudly confirmed that he had masterminded the Knightsbridge job. It was said with typical Viccei gusto and showmanship and summed up this master criminal's mentality. He told the courtroom: "I am the person responsible for the entire operation of the 12 July. I conceived it, planned it, organized it, physically carried it out and finally managed the sale phase."

Not surprisingly, Viccei's highly publicized capture at the wheel of his Ferrari turned him into something of an underworld folk hero. "The Italian Stallion", "The Wolf", "The Gentleman Thief" – he exulted in all these nicknames.

In real life, though, his family background was far more respectable. He was the son of a libel lawyer and boutique-owning mother from Ascoli Piceno, near Rome. Viccei had craved adulation since childhood and he never hesitated to use violence in order to achieve it.

A thief by 16, he went to university in Rome to study philosophy in the 1970s, but fell under the influence of the neo-Fascist terrorist leader Gianni Nardi. Viccei joined the youth group *Fronte della Giuventù*, daubing swastikas on public buildings before graduating to bombings. As politics became a distant motive, he racked up a suspected 54 robberies in Italy.

Viccei even proudly modeled himself on the hit movie *Scarface*, starring Al Pacino, which he had reputedly watched 58 times. He even had a gold keyring in the shape of a shotgun. The combination number for his £700 Louis Vuitton briefcase was 357, after the .357 Magnum that he often carried. In London, he didn't allow broken English to inhibit him from chasing women or committing numerous armed robberies before he targeted the Knightsbridge Safety Deposit Centre.

And after his capture for the Knightsbridge job, Viccei continued to play the master villain. Suave and athletic, with his sunglasses, permanent grin, jokes and boasts. Newspapers drooled over his cunning and charm.

Others were not so impressed. "I found him boring, showing off his Rolex watch and talking about his fast cars," recalled Justine Marr, secretary to Parvez Latif, who owned the safe deposit centre and whom Viccei befriended and trapped into helping him commit the raid.

One of the detectives who arrested Viccei was equally dismissive: "He wanted to be known as the mastermind of the world's biggest robbery. He has an ego the size of the Old Bailey."

It mattered not. A star was born. Viccei even told the judge at his eventual trial for the Knightsbridge job: "Maybe I am a romantic lunatic but money was the last thing on my mind."

Only £10 million of the £40 million stolen at the Knightsbridge Safe Deposit centre was ever recovered.

Viccei was eventually sentenced to 22 years for his part in the heist. When he was in prison, he even wore a T-shirt emblazoned with the slogan "I love Knightsbridge" around a clown's face with dollar signs for eyes.

Viccei's partner in the Knightsbridge job, Rubin, avoided arrest for years until he eventually returned to Britain in 1990 and received a 12-year sentence for his role in the heist. "Inside man" Latif was sentenced to 16 years.

Viccei was full of praise for Parkhurst Jail, the island prison on the Isle of Wight. He later wrote in his memoirs: "I never expected an English prison to be as good as this, and I am saying so in all honesty. People's perceptions about prison life are very unreal and whereas some are prone to believe that it is pure hell, some maintain it is too soft and totally inadequate for our sins. The truth, as usual, has to be found in the middle and everybody should realize that conditions vary hugely from one prison to another."

Viccei and the lead detective who arrested him in his Ferrari, Dick Leach, went on to form an unlikely friendship and Leach was even able to persuade Viccei to reveal the whereabouts of some of the Knightsbridge spoils, along with crucial information about a series of gangland executions and the 1982 murder in London of "God's Banker" Roberto Calvi.

Viccei and Leach regularly wrote letters to each other, in which Viccei always referred to Leach as "Fred" – after the bloodhound Fred Bassett – and himself as "Garfield" or "The Wolf". Viccei's friendly relationship with Leach came as a result of the way Leach had treated and respected Viccei's family and girlfriend, Helle Skoubon, following his arrest. Leach explained: "They were very important to him and I treated them courteously so he would open up to me. He also wanted visits from his family, which we allowed."

Skoubon was convicted of handling stolen property and got a suspended sentence just after Viccei was sentenced.

Viccei told Leach he had committed up to five London robberies, although he never named any of his accomplices. "He was a man of his word and didn't want to lose respect," recalled the detective.

Viccei's final police record included a total of 54 robberies; the 1981 murder of an accomplice to which he confessed in 1993; blowing up a broadcasting transmitter at the age of 17;

and stealing a Fiat 500 to go to a neo-Fascist rally in Rome, which had earned him his first arrest. But behind the scenes, Viccei was quietly working away at trying to get a transfer back home to Italy to serve out the remainder of his sentence. Not surprisingly, he felt he'd have much more power and influence in an Italian prison. Also, his family and numerous other criminal contacts would be nearby.

Viccei's lawyer told the authorities that he was determined to exercise his right to serve out the rest of his sentence in his home country. The UK authorities were reluctant at first, until it was pointed out that it made more sense for Viccei's incarceration to be paid for by the country of his birth.

Viccei was finally allowed to return to Italy in November 1992, under the Treaty of Strasbourg agreement. He was transferred from Parkhurst to a jail in Pescara on the Adriatic coast to complete his sentence. He was careful not to sneer at the UK authorities, but Viccei knew that he was as good as free at a prison in Italy, unlike when he was in Britain.

Within three years, Viccei was confidently strolling the beachside cafés on his way to work at a publisher's office, thanks to a special arrangement with the prison which enabled Viccei to have a legitimate "day job" – as long as he returned to jail at 10.30pm every night.

Viccei tried to disguise the glee he felt about his new "freedom" by publicly insisting: "The legal system in Italy may look softer than Britain's, but it is not. The only difference is that the rehabilitation programme does not discriminate like it does in Britain."

An autobiography written inside jail seemed to help that rehabilitation (and his bank balance), but Viccei was never the type simply to slide into obscurity. He was effectively living in the outside world on a permanent day-release "pass" and was free for to do as he pleased for 12 hours a day.

Back in the UK, detectives and prison officials alike tried to laugh off the "easy life" Viccei was so obviously leading in Italy by saying it was typical of the notorious robber that he'd manipulated such a cushy life for himself, despite the fact that he was supposed to be under lock and key until his scheduled parole in 2003. However, they made no complaints to the Italian authorities. "He was their problem now, so we all kind of stepped back," explained one detective who had taken part in Viccei's dramatic arrest at Marble Arch.

During this period, Viccei befriended Antonio Malatesta, a member of the Puglia Mafia, known as the "Sacred United Heart", which specialized in kidnappings, armed hold-ups and smuggling. Malatesta was also free to roam the streets near the prison while serving time because he'd become a supergrass (a *pentito*), which in Italy was a fast track to reduced sentences and privileges.

Italian justice had made supergrasses and rapid releases for "model prisoners" central to its fight against organized crime. Since the first Mafioso had broken the code of *omertà* in the 1980s and started talking, thousands of others had followed suit. It sometimes seemed as if the Italian justice system was specifically built to accommodate such notorious inmates as luxuriously as possible.

By the year 2000, Viccei's day release from jail in Pescara was enabling him to live the sort of carefree lifestyle he'd long been accustomed to. Now a silver-haired, sharp-suited figure, he looked like a wealthy businessman. He now even owned and ran his own translation company in the nearest town.

Law enforcement officials back in the UK continued to struggle with the idea that one of the most notorious blaggers in criminal history had managed to persuade the authorities to allow him so much freedom that he was able to socialize with the Mafia. There were rumours that Viccei was bribing prison officials, but nothing concrete. As usual, Viccei was flaunting his freedom – and no one seemed able to stop him.

At 11.30am on the morning of 19 April 2000, Valerio Viccei, now 44 years old, had a "business meeting" with his Mafia gangster associate Malatesta in an isolated country lane. The two men were standing by a Lancia Thema parked on a dirt track near the town of Ascoli, when a police patrol car stumbled on them.

The officers were immediately suspicious and a call to base quickly revealed the Lancia to be stolen. Officer Enzo Baldini then stepped from his patrol car and crunched over the gravel towards Viccei.

Baldini was 30 feet away when Viccei raised his beloved semi-automatic Magnum .357 handgun and fired. The first shot missed, but three others soon followed. The policeman crumpled as one bullet tore into his leg. Baldini grasped his sub-machine gun as the figure with the gun continued racing towards him. Baldini then loosed off 15 rounds and his assailant twirled and toppled. There was no scream; Viccei was dead before he hit the ground.

Viccei's body had been literally riddled with bullets from the policeman's automatic weapon. In the chaos that followed, Maletesta dragged Viccei's body into the car and sped off. But when Maletesta realized his associate was dead, he dumped Viccei's bullet-riddled corpse out of the speeding car. Police later discovered Viccei's body on a road in Teramo, 100 miles east of Rome.

Reinforcements arrived at the scene and dozens of police gathered around the corpse. No one recognized him. The master robber was initially mistaken for an Albanian bandit. A detective, who'd known Viccei for most of his adult life, finally confirmed his identity some hours later. By Viccei's own criterion, he died a failure: "The rule of this game is that if they don't catch you, you are a genius. But if they do, you are a miserable nobody," he wrote in his best-selling memoirs.

The Lancia Thema was later found dumped by a quiet B-road behind some bushes. In the boot police discovered two carnival masks, a police bat used to halt traffic and a police-issue overhead flashing light.

The police believed Viccei and Maletesta were planning to either rob a bank security van or kidnap a member of one of the area's three industrialist families. For a career criminal like Viccei, such a plan would have been impossible to resist. It wasn't just about greed. Criminality was etched in his blood. He could never resist an opportunity to put two fingers up to society.

Viccei had even been wearing gloves when he died, showing, Italian police said, that the lesson he had been taught in London – he was nailed for the Knightsbridge robbery thanks to a fingerprint – had remained forever etched in his mind.

AFTERMATH

Following the shootout, speculation was rife in the Italian press that Viccei might have been set up by police, whom he had been a thorn in the side of for so many years until he went to Britain and pulled off the Knightsbridge job. The Italian cops had been frustrated by Viccei's own admission that he'd carried out at least 50 bank raids in Italy. They felt humiliated by him. But then again, it was no surprise that Viccei was armed on that cloudy April day when he met his maker. He even told one associate many years earlier: "You know I am fascinated with guns. When I was in Italy I felt undressed without them."

Viccei himself had long claimed he had many enemies among Italy's police and criminal fraternity. Viccei even confessed while in prison to killing a rival gangster ten years before he pulled off the Knightsbridge robbery. He said: "I was alerted that this guy was looking for me with a gun. I found him first and he became history. I had no option. If I had not taken him out, I would not be here today. My friends disposed of his body."

Yet Viccei's death leaves one huge unanswered question: why would he bother to commit more crimes when he still had millions of pounds from the Knightsbridge job?

The answer lies in something that had been a recurring feature throughout Viccei's entire life: the buzz, the excitement. As previously touched upon, Viccei was addicted to crime. It wasn't about the money. He craved the "hits" of excitement that crime provided and when he needed another injection of adrenaline, he simply went out and got it.

Ex-Flying squad officer Dick Leach – who'd befriended Viccei in prison – later said: "He needed the buzz and excitement of robbing – and look how he ended up. There's no place in the sun for him. It goes to show that crime's a mug's game. Viccei just couldn't leave it alone. Crime was a power trip for him and had nothing to do with money. But I was still saddened by his death. He was a one-off character."

Viccei himself once said: "I always wanted to reach something that was top of its field." But then he was at the peak of his glamour and infamy – a lifetime away from the moment a terrified traffic cop became his nemesis. His death shook Italy. Viccei was not supposed to be sitting armed in a stolen car waiting to ambush a bank security van. He was still technically serving time, but had been allowed out during the day to work in a publisher's office.

Just before Viccei's final, deadly showdown with the police, he told his Italian lawyer he'd reached a verbal agreement with a British producer for a movie to be made about his life.

Viccei, who would have been due for parole just three years later, was proud of his criminal expertise. It's ironic that if he'd stayed in prison in the UK he would probably still be alive today. As Viccei himself once said: "I have lived by the gun, and maybe one day I'll die by the gun."

7. POINTING THE FINGER

"I wasn't involved in any conspiracy to commit robbery."

Securicor van driver **Graham Huckerby**

Midland Clearing Centre, Salford, Greater Manchester,
3 July 1995, 8am

A sk any blagger what he's really after and he'll tell you "cash is the name of the game". Robbers can sit on unmarked notes for years if they want to. One old-time robber recently told me: "Gold, traveller's cheques, jewellery. None of it is half as valuable as cash when it comes to the crunch."

No doubt this was very much on the minds of the masked raiders who lay in wait for a Securicor van to make an early morning delivery to the Midland Bank district service centre in Salford, Greater Manchester.

As the bulletproof van swept into the centre's yard to deposit weekend takings from the big Manchester stores, two masked men used ladders to scale a wall next to a nearby railway line and dropped into the centre of the yard.

They moved silently and menacingly towards the van moments after the driver's colleague had got out of the vehicle and walked into the building to check in their delivery.

Suddenly a masked man armed with a gun knocked on the window and demanded that the driver let him in, saying they were holding his colleague hostage. Driver Graham Huckerby's training told him always to put people before money, so he agreed. He thought the rest of the gang had bundled his colleague into the back of the van.

Huckerby, 31, was terrified. Only a few months earlier he'd witnessed another colleague being hit over the head with a sledgehammer and stabbed in the chest during another robbery attempt.

Huckerby later said he was so scared he wet himself and that was why he failed to raise any alarm. So, with a masked man pointing a gun to his head, he drove off, followed by the gang's stolen white Transit van. The robber instructed Huckerby to drive to a nearby cul-de-sac at the end of Hope Street, Salford, and then to stop the van behind the Salford Fire Station. When he had done so, he was bound and gagged.

Then the raiders pulled Huckerby out of the vehicle and dragged him to a lamppost, to which they handcuffed him while two of the blaggers began speedily transferring cash bags and boxes out of the Securicor vehicle. In all, 29 pillowcase-sized cash bags were thrown into the robbers' white Transit. Within two minutes, the robbers had jumped in the Transit – knowing how quickly the police would be alerted to the crime, the blaggers, sticking to their strict schedule, left £1 million behind – and were en route to another rendezvous. There, the gang moved the cash to another vehicle and then scattered in a fleet of stolen cars.

A workman who saw Huckerby being handcuffed to the railings alerted police, but they arrived long after the gang had departed with all the loot. The robbers' white Transit van was later found abandoned with its number plates missing.

Not surprisingly, many old pros in the UK underworld sat up and took notice of the Salford "job". It had been a carefully orchestrated raid during which the gang had escaped with £6.6 million in cash. What's more, none of that £6.6 million would ever be recovered.

As one old-time robber told me years later: "Not bad for a day's work, eh?"

Securicor immediately offered a reward of £250,000 for information leading to arrests in connection with the robbery. A spokesman for the company told reporters: "Securicor takes all incidents extremely seriously, as the safety of its staff and the public is of paramount importance. Securicor is doing everything possible to assist the police with their investigations."

The Midland Bank service centre specialized in processing branch vouchers from all over the north-west of England. A spokeswoman for the bank reassured customers that any disruption would be kept to a minimum. "Branches keep back-up copies of all transactions," she said. "And many of the transactions contained on the vouchers would already have been put straight into the computer system."

CCTV cameras positioned in the yard of the depot caught

the entire raid and the police hoped they might get some vital clues after the footage was examined. Within hours of the blagging, detectives had interviewed witnesses including security van driver Graham Huckerby and issued a description of at least three robbers. One was said to be wearing a blue anorak, was 5 feet 6–7 inches tall and spoke with a strong Irish accent. Another was of mixed race, 6 feet tall and slim and spoke with a northern accent. The third was 5 feet 9–10 inches tall and wore black trousers and a black anorak.

It also emerged that the raid had been one of a number of violent robberies carried out in Salford over the previous ten months, although police insisted they were not linking the crimes. The first had taken place in October 1994, when two security guards had been attacked outside a supermarket in Hankinson Way, Pendleton, and robbed of £11,000. The following February a woman had been abducted after a bungled robbery next to a Sainsbury's superstore close to the Midland Bank service centre. The assailant had even opened fire to warn off pursuing staff. A month later, two gunmen and a third robber kidnapped a security guard as he emerged from a nearby supermarket and escaped with £60,000 in a cash box. It seemed that the Salford area was rife with violent armed robbers.

But as police began to unravel the facts behind the previous robberies, they became highly suspicious of Securicor driver Graham Huckerby, because he had been the victim of one of the earlier robberies as well. Always on the lookout for an obvious "inside man", police made Huckerby their prime suspect for the Midland Bank job.

One of the recurring features of virtually all the heists

featured in this book is the existence of an alleged inside man; most robbers and the police see him as the key to any blagging. So it was hardly surprising that Salford police were utterly convinced that the robbery could not have been carried out without someone "opening doors" for the blaggers. And that "someone" was Graham Huckerby.

Many detectives to this day believe that most robberies will fail without an inside man. They like to cite the later 2000 Millennium Dome robbery as a classic example. "It was just a glorified ram-raid," says one ex-Flying Squad detective.

Detectives investigating the Salford job suspected that Huckerby had been targeted by members of the gang and had then been "persuaded" to co-operate with them and provide the villains with essential inside information, as well as not fighting them off when they came to hijack his van.

The police argument both back then and now is that it's hardly surprising that workers at banks and cash depots can be "turned", as most of them are paid a minimum wage for their duties.

But police have also always believed that such inside men could be a gang's Achilles heel, as has been the case in numerous heists down the years, the Brink's-Mat job (see pages 103–34), for example.

So police investigating the Salford heist refused to believe Huckerby's protestations of innocence. In fact, the more he denied having had any involvement with the gang, the more they believed he was a guilty man.

But without a confession and with no other suspects for the actual robbery, police needed more concrete evidence on Huckerby if they were going to nail him. Huckerby's apparent "guilt" was further compounded when Securicor suspended and then dismissed him within a month of the robbery. Surely that meant they knew he was guilty? No smoke without fire seemed to be the clear implication.

So police investigating the Salford blagging launched Operation Volga to ensure the case remained "live" until the gang were brought to justice. Detectives even engaged an undercover policeman, known only as "Barry", to go to pubs and bookmakers in the area where Huckerby lived and prove his connection to the robbery.

The operation took months to get going and eventually lasted two years. It was specifically designed to see if any of Huckerby's associates were involved in similar crimes. Eventually, the police's undercover officer had tape-recorded conversations that he claimed were evidence that another robbery was being planned and which provided proof that Huckerby was involved in blaggings.

Now three years after the actual robbery had taken place, police believed they finally had the evidence to convict Huckerby and a colleague, and both men were arrested for their alleged role in a robbery conspiracy. Huckerby was stunned and steadfastly maintained his innocence. This surprised detectives because inside men usually crumbled once they were presented with concrete evidence. Finally, in 2002, both Huckerby and his associate were put on trial for their involvement in the robbery conspiracy.

During the trial it was alleged that Huckerby had taken a £1,000 bribe to let the masked gunmen hijack his bullet- and bombproof Securicor vehicle, kidnap him and steal the £6.6 million. It was further alleged that Huckerby had spun a web of deceit, telling police he had been "terrified" at being kidnapped and held against his will.

Police also alleged that they'd been tipped off that the raid had been organized by one of London's most notorious gangsters, who in turn had recruited Greater Manchester hoodlums to carry out "the job". Those "hoodlums", claimed the police, allegedly included Huckerby and his associate.

Huckerby, 41 at the time of the trial, also denied taking a £1,000 "sweetener" from the robbers before the blagging was carried out. Huckerby told the court: "I did not fall prey to any temptation… I did not take £1,000 from anyone as a sweetener. I was not involved in any robbery in any shape, fashion or form. There is no secret stash of cash, because I wasn't involved in any conspiracy to commit robbery."

However prosecuting counsel Martin Steiger QC accused Huckerby of being "financially stretched" in late 1994 just before the robbery. Steiger told the court Huckerby owed maintenance for his ex-wife and child and his overdraft facilities had been temporarily closed.

The court also heard that, following the Salford raid, Huckerby took a three-week holiday to California and made a series of cash deposits in his account of up to £500 at a time. Huckerby admitted exceeding his overdraft facilities in 1994, but declared: "I wasn't under financial pressure and I wasn't struggling that much. If I had needed money, I would have gone to my mum and dad and they would have always helped me out."

He admitted taking out a £1,000 loan in October 1994, but said it was to help a friend's security business venture. His mother paid off his maintenance arrears. Huckerby said the cash deposits made after the robbery were installments of a £3,500 loan being paid back to him by a friend. He also denied prosecuting counsel Steiger's suggestions that he went out socializing "time and time again" after the robbery.

But despite Huckerby and his associate's consistent denials, the jury returned a unanimous verdict of conspiracy to rob after the two-month trial. As Huckerby and his associate were each jailed for 14 years, Huckerby sank to his knees at the Minshull Street Crown Court, in Manchester, and shouted, "What have you done to me?"

Even from their prison cells, Huckerby and his associate continued to insist they were completely innocent and accused the police of framing them simply because they presumed Huckerby had been the inside man involved in the robbery. The police, meanwhile, dismissed Huckerby's pleas as typical of those of a man found guilty of a major crime. But Huckerby believed he had evidence that would get the verdict against him and his associate overthrown. For more than a year, both men worked with their lawyers putting together an appeal.

AFTERMATH

In December 2004, both men's cases were heard at London's Court of Appeal. Huckerby's lawyers provided medical proof to the court that he'd only co-operated with the robbers because of the post-traumatic stress he had suffered from the robbery that had taken place seven months before the Salford heist. That was why he did what the robbers told him to when they had pointed a gun at him.

The Court of Appeal judges quashed both men's conviction saying: "We are not satisfied as to the safety of the conviction." Lord Justice Potter said it was "in the interests of justice" to consider the new medical evidence about Huckerby's state of mind during the robbery. "Having done so, we are not satisfied as to the safety of the conviction," he concluded.

The court also set aside confiscation orders made against the two men of £50,000 each or 15 months in prison. According to the judgment, it was crystal clear that neither Huckerby nor his friend had any connection to the Salford blagging, or any other robbery for that matter.

Among Huckerby's supporters had been the campaigning groups *Innocent* and the *Miscarriages of Justice Organization (MOJO)*. Dr Andrew Green, a criminologist who founded *Innocent*, said they agreed with police that the raid had involved an insider, but always maintained they'd simply got the wrong man. "The fact the police have got absolutely no one for this crime and have not recovered a penny of the money seems a gross failure of the criminal justice system," said Dr Green.

Campaigning journalist Don Hale also played a pivotal role in helping secure Huckerby's release. Hale had being asked to investigate the case by his family. Hale met Huckerby at Dovegate prison, visited the scenes of the robbery and interviewed several witnesses.

After Huckerby's acquittal, Hale said: "I was able to cast doubt on the conviction by providing credible evidence to counter the original claims at trial, and even proved Huckerby had been the victim of another raid several months before when his van was again attacked and his colleague stabbed. I was determined to campaign for justice and I am so pleased that both men are to be released."

Despite the four-year investigation, Operation Volga did not result in the capture of any robbers or the recovery of any of the money. As master robber Freddie Foreman said: "Job well done."

8. OPERATION MAGICIAN

"They were a ruthless team of criminals who set out to commit the largest robbery ever to take place anywhere in the world."

Scotland Yard police detective

Greenwich, London, 7 November 2000

The De Beers Millennium Collection – a dozen diamonds valued at between £200 million and £350 million, including the world's most perfect gem, the 203-carat Millennium Star – played a leading role in London's Thames-side Millennium Dome celebrations to mark the start of the new century. Hundreds of millions of TV viewers across the globe watched as high-powered laser beams were directed at the gems, which filled the building with sparkling shafts of light. It was, in the words of many, a magnificent sight.

"That's the one!" yelled a drunken Raymond Betson, 40, as he watched the New Year extravaganza on TV at home in nearby Kent that night. "That's the one I want and I'm gonna 'ave it!"

Betson, a not very successful "career criminal", was fed up with scraping together a living ducking and diving through the dodgy world of VAT fraud and illegal shipments of cigarettes from Spain.

Over the next few months, Betson became, in the words of one associate, like a man possessed. He kept thinking about those diamonds sitting there in the Dome just waiting to be stolen. But inside the criminal hinterlands of south-east London – from where Betson originated – many folk considered the gems to be "legitimate targets". Betson also wanted what all criminals crave for: underworld infamy and enough untold riches to retire forever. But as most hoods will admit during their darkest (or most drunken) moments: "Crime never really pays".

Meanwhile, Betson convinced himself that, if he was going to pull off the biggest robbery in the world, he would need the right criminal connections – and the financial backing – to put together a "team". He went to see one of south London's most notorious gangsters and persuaded him to advance enough cash to set up the job. In return, *Mr Big* also assured Betson that not only was he prepared to "invest" some cash in the planning of the job, but he'd also line up some particularly heavyweight Russians to "take the gems off yer hands".

Betson was delighted with the arrangement, because even he had to admit he "didn't have a fucking clue" what to do with the gems once he had them in his hands.

On 1 September 2000, Betson and his best friend William

Cockram, 49, and associate Aldo Ciarrocchi, 32, visited the Dome for the first time. Cockram headed straight to the Money Zone, where he concentrated on the De Beers Millennium Diamond Exhibition and filmed the vault with a camcorder. The De Beers diamond exhibition had a number of jewels on display as well as that same Millennium Star, a flawless 203.04-carat (40.61g) gem with an estimated worth of £200 million and considered one of the most perfect gems in the world. Mined in the Democratic Republic of Congo in 1992, it was rated "a perfect diamond with absolutely no flaws" and had weighed 777 carats before it was cut.

The Millennium Star was on display in a specially built, £50,000 cabinet that featured three-quarters-of-an-inch-thick reinforced glass and sophisticated security systems. In a similar cabinet nearby were 11 blue diamonds that De Beers had owned since 1890 and which were regarded as unique because of their shape and colour. Having secretly filmed them all on his camera, Cockram then met up with Betson nearby and the pair videoed the river and jetty surrounding the Dome. They were later joined by Ciarrocchi, and reviewed the earlier recorded footage and studied a plan of the Dome's layout.

The gang's most difficult problem would be to overcome those "impregnable" diamond display cases. Built to resist the force of a 60-ton ram raid, the explosive-resistant glass was also designed to foil any "known tool" for at least 30 minutes. However, robber Cockram believed he had the answer. He reckoned he could weaken the glass with three shots from a powerful Hilti nail-gun. Then they would use a sledgehammer to break the "warmed" glass.

The key storage location for the gang's robbery equipment while they prepared for the robbery was the Old Coal Yard in Whitehart Road, Plumstead, south-east London. The yard housed a disused Railtrack engine shed as well as a yellow JCB mechanical digger, stolen some months earlier, which would play a pivotal role in the robbery as the gang's battering ram. The robbers believed that a digger would not attract unwelcome attention near the Dome because of constant building work that was going in the area. They also rented two remote farms near Maidstone, in Kent, to use as flophouses after the robbery.

More visits to the Dome followed and, in late September 2000, gang member Terry Millman, 57 – who was suffering from cancer – used the name "T. Diamond" when he handed over £3,700 in cash to buy a speedboat at a yard in the seaside town of Whitstable, Kent, after testing it carefully.

The gang used pay-as-you-go mobile phones to arrange meetings during all their reconnaissance trips. Team members even posed as tourists with their families to re-film the gems in the Money Zone. Ammonia gas was purchased – to knock out any potential "have-a-go heroes" – and smoke bombs were bought to ensure chaos if they were "rumbled" while the robbery was being carried out.

On three separate days gang members towed the Kent-based speedboat to Greenwich and placed it on the river opposite the Dome. Other activity on those days further indicated that the actual robbery was imminent.

Then the raid itself was aborted on two occasions. On 6 October 2000 the speedboat developed engine problems. A second attempt a few days later was cut short because the

Thames tide was too low for the gang to use the boat as a getaway.

The tide on the River Thames fluctuates on a fortnightly cycle. The tide had to be at its highest possible level for the speedboat to be launched on the north side of the river. The next optimum time for the robbery to take place was on 7 November 2000.

Unfortunately for Betson and his gang, however, the Art of Police Detection was about to super-cede the so-called Art of Robbery.

At 3am on 7 November 2000, approximately 200 police officers gathered at the Dome for a dawn briefing. They were prepared for a tactical operation, which had been months in the planning and provided contingencies for many different outcomes. Public safety was the prime consideration and officers had plans to ensure that the robbers could be arrested quickly and safely at any given stage during the attempted heist.

Among those present were 40 specialist firearms officers. Some of them would be hidden behind a secret wall within the Dome. Others were sent into the Dome in disguise. Dressed as cleaners, they concealed their guns in black plastic bags and rubbish bins. Surveillance officers disguised as Dome employees also patrolled the area to hamper any escape attempts. The police used the Millennium Dome's CCTV room as a control room.

A further 60 armed Flying Squad officers were stationed around the Thames and 20 on the river itself. Officers also moved to a number of observation points between the robbers' "depot" at the Old Coal Yard in Plumstead and the Dome. The police operation to foil the raiders had been codenamed "Operation Magician" and was commanded by the Flying Squad's Detective Superintendent Jon Shatford.

The robbers had no idea their every move had been watched by police for more than a month.

At 9.00am on 7 November, a speedboat glided up to Queen Elizabeth jetty on the Thames and cut its two engines to avoid drawing attention.

On the other side of the river at the Dome site, four men posing as builders unloaded the JCB, preparing, it seemed, for work on a nearby site. They revved up the digger noisily so that the 60-odd visitors already touring the Dome took little notice of the "construction workers".

At 9.30am, the gang, armed with a nail-gun, a hammer, smoke bombs and, bizarrely, a Catherine-wheel firework made their audacious and extraordinary move. They believed no one would dare get in their way.

The digger clattered at full pelt into the wire fence, crushing it flat before startled security guards. It then charged towards the Dome's Money Zone. In the mayhem, four masked men slipped inside the perimeter before two of them slipped through the narrow door of the diamond vault and headed for what they thought was the Millennium Star, a diamond so distinctive it could never be sold on the open market.

Betson and his associate Ciarrocchi remained outside while Cockram and another gang member Robert Adams, 58, headed into the vault.

Police surrounding the building immediately moved in and arrested the outside team, knowing that their two vault men would be none the wiser.

Inside the vault, Bill Cockram was filmed by a secret police surveillance video with his nose pressed against the glass like a boy outside Hamleys at Christmas. He then looked for a plastic interlayer, which sat between two sheets of glass to protect it from a smash-and-grab attack. There was none. That meant Cockram and Adams could smash a fist-sized hole in the double-thickness glass. By their reckoning the world's most fabulous collection of diamonds would be in their hands within 30 seconds.

They were, in fact, looking at a replica: all the diamonds had been replaced with crystal copies the day before, following a police request.

And, once inside that vault, the robbers had effectively imprisoned themselves within the 4 feet concrete walls. Without a lookout standing guard, they began viciously smashing the reinforced glass cases with hammers, sledgehammers and electric nailguns.

"I was 12 inches from pay day," Adams later said. "It would have been a blinding Christmas."

The gang had planned to be in their 55mph speedboat speeding across the Thames to a rendezvous with Russian gangsters at the Mayflower pub in Rotherhithe within three minutes of grabbing the diamonds. Instead, two minutes into the raid, they were ambushed by 200 armed police, who threw distraction devices into the vault and then entered and overpowered the pair and ordered the robbers to drop their weapons and come out. Neither men put up any resistance.

Gotcha!

As detectives handcuffed robber Adams, they noticed a strong smell of ammonia and discovered that both Adams and Cockram were carrying bottles of the substance. Betson and Ciarrocchi were already handcuffed and laid out on the tarmac outside.

As one member of the gang ruefully put it: "We would have got away with it but for the fact there were 200 police waiting for us."

Outside the Dome, armed officers deployed on three boats left their hiding places and moved towards Millennium Pier. They quickly cut off "boatman" Kevin Meredith's escape route and arrested him. Meredith was carrying a large quantity of petrol, which police believed would have been used to set fire to the boat after they had delivered the diamonds to the waiting Russian gangsters.

A sixth man was monitoring the police's movements on a shortwave radio on the north side of the River Thames at the Lower Lea Crossing. He was parked a white Ford Transit van, which had been seen towing the speedboat earlier that morning.

Ozcan Ocak, who worked at the Dome at the time, later recalled: "I heard a terrible crashing noise as if there was an accident. When I went out to look I saw a bulldozer outside going through the Money Zone. There were police everywhere at the time. We did not take it seriously for a moment, but then the police told us to get back."

Ocak continued: "I felt a sense of disbelief. It was like something out of a movie. Someone next to me even asked whether this was part of the live entertainment at the Dome. There was smoke all over the area. You could smell gunpowder right up your nostrils."

Security staff rushed visitors away from the Money Zone

and a party of schoolchildren from Surrey huddled in a room and sang hymns to keep their spirits up. Earlier that morning, London Underground had been ordered to shut North Greenwich station, which served the Dome, at the request of Scotland Yard. The London Ambulance Service was put on standby to "expect casualties".

Another eyewitness who was with a group of school children from Dorset said he was alerted by loud crashing noises. He explained: "All the kids were having a meal in McDonald's when there was a loud bang. I heard what sounded like automatic gunfire. When we were allowed back out, there was a JCB digger parked by the Money Zone."

At the scene of the police swoop, David James – then the Dome's executive chairman – watched in amazement as the robbers lay on the ground trussed up "like Christmas turkeys". He later recalled: "It was relatively calm and they were almost joking with the police who were standing over them with guns."

As Betson, Aldo Ciarrocchi, Bob "The Builder" Adams and Bill Cockram lay trussed up and joking with the armed officers standing over them, just 100 yards to their right, 50 Miss World hopefuls were having a photo-call. A party of tourists from Devon was also complaining to a bemused policeman that they were seriously miffed to have missed it.

Detective Superintendent Jon Shatford defended the decision to wait until the gang had reached the diamonds before arresting them. He said: "Our chief concern throughout was public safety. We decided it was better to let the robbers get to the vault where they were effectively imprisoned."

The blaggers were eventually taken to different police stations in south-east London for questioning. The following day, 8 November, they were all charged. Meanwhile, the following morning, Kent police's serious crime unit, working in conjunction with Scotland Yard, arrested six more people in connection with the raid the following morning. These arrests were made in the Kent villages of Collier Street and Horsmonden.

The Dome "bust" was one of the Flying Squad's finest moments. They'd had the gang members under surveillance for its suspected roles in a number of previous unsuccessful armoured-vehicle robberies and had then "stumbled" on the blaggers' main target – the Dome. The operation to foil the robbery was the biggest mission undertaken in the Flying Squad's checkered history and at the robbers' eventual trial the judge made a special point of commending the way the police handled the operation.

Detectives believe to this day that the "Dome Raiders" were stealing to order for the Russian Mafia, who in turn were acting for a wealthy collector, possibly an Arab.

Diamond experts speculated that the robbers were working for a syndicate, ultimately in the Middle East, that would cut the diamonds into smaller rocks before selling them. Another possibility was that the robbers were unaware of how difficult it would be to dispose of such distinctive diamonds, even on the black market.

The police operation itself – codenamed Operation Magician – had been set up in total secrecy. The Cabinet Office and senior figures in the New Millennium Experience Company and the mining company De Beers, which owned the diamonds, had been informed. The Commissioner of the Metropolitan Police, Sir John Stevens, had also been briefed.

The Flying Squad had no doubt the Millennium Raid would have been the biggest robbery since the Brink's-Mat raid at Heathrow in 1983. Detective Superintendent Shatford told a press conference after the swoop: "Had this been carried out in accordance with their wishes, it would have been the largest robbery in the world. It was a very audacious robbery attempt, but was foiled by an even more audacious police response. The minute the individuals made an overt attempt to commit the robbery they were arrested with overwhelming force. Tactically this was an extremely difficult operation and it took a great deal of planning. Our paramount concern throughout was the threat to the public."

Asked why the police had not stepped in before the gang reached the Money Zone, Shatford said: "The biggest danger would have been to let them escape or frustrate them before they could commit the offence. We have to produce the best evidence. If we fail to do that we are letting the public down because we are saying it is too difficult for us and we will let them go and commit crime elsewhere. The planning we went through and the result vindicates the strategy used."

Executives from the New Millennium Experience Company, which ran the Dome, made it clear they would have preferred to avoid the police showdown. One said: "The police asked us to collaborate and this is a public building so they took over. It was a police operation, so they made the calls. We had no choice. My worst nightmare was for someone to be hurt. I haven't slept very well these past few weeks."

Andrew Lamont, a spokesman for De Beers, said the company had been first told of the risk to the diamonds in September, when floor plans for the display were stolen from the dome.

An anonymous caller offered to return the plans for money, but De Beers called the police. "At this point, we were informed by Scotland Yard that they were already investigating a possible threat to the display," explained Mr Lamont.

Scotland Yard later insisted that the theft of the plans was "completely separate" to the failed robbery.

Mr Lamont also said that cutting up the Millennium Star would be "like cutting up a Van Gogh or Monet. It would only be worth a tiny fraction of the whole."

The "Dome Raiders" – as they became known in the tabloids – came to trial at the Old Bailey a year later on 8 November 2001, but only six members of the gang were present as, in the intervening period, Terry Millman had died of cancer.

Prosecuting counsel Martin Heslop opened the case against the six robbers by telling the court: "The value of the diamonds is conservatively estimated – and I pause before giving you the figure – at £200 million. Had they succeeded, it would have ranked in terms of value as the biggest robbery ever in the world and could perhaps be described as the robbery of the millennium.

"The operation was planned professionally, carefully and down to the last detail and was so well organized that it would probably have succeeded and they would have probably got away with it had it not been for an equally professional, careful and detailed police operation."

Mr Heslop told the court the gang faced a number of difficulties, not least the extensive security at the Dome and De Beers's own security arrangements.

"No doubt an armoured tank would have suited their purpose," Mr Heslop said. "But they chose the JCB, which could approach the Dome without arousing suspicion because of building work. It had also been specially adapted to carry four of the raiders and when driven at speed was very frightening.

"They could use this force and power to smash their way into the Dome and approach the vault. It would cause terror to those outside as it approached. Then it could transport them at speed by the quickest route."

Mr Heslop told the court that an associate of the gang bought a farmhouse and surrounding orchards in Kent early in early 2000 for £350,000. Once detectives came to suspect there might be a plan to steal the diamonds, the farmhouse was watched and stolen vehicles were seen driven into the property.

The JCB was also spotted at that farmhouse as well as at another farm – ten minutes' drive away – used by the gang. It was there that two speedboats were also seen. One was discarded as unreliable and the second, capable of doing 55mph, was chosen instead.

On the first day of the defence case, alleged robber William Cockram told the court about the lack of security inside the Dome. "I couldn't believe how simple it was. I was thinking, this cannot be true. It was a gift. At first I had thought it was pie in the sky, but after going down there I couldn't believe the security was so bad… There was nobody in the vault, no security workers walking around." He stated that, had the plan succeeded, "It would have taken a very short time from hitting the main gate to getting back across the Thames – five minutes maximum." Cockram also insisted: "No one was going to get hurt; there was no one to hurt, because the Dome was always empty."

Cockram also claimed that the nail-gun the gang bought was to be used to break the glass in the vault and *not* as a weapon. The ammonia, he said, was to be used to contaminate any traces of blood left by the two raiders in the vault. He explained that the body armour he wore was to be used after the raid for protection when he was scheduled to attend a meeting with associates to discuss the sale of the gems.

Fellow robber Betson claimed that his brother-in-law PC Michael Waring – who was working at the Dome as part of the perimeter security – had tipped him off about the lax security at the Dome through a school friend named Tony, who was also working at the Dome. Betson claimed that Waring had told him about a plan that Tony had put together to steal the gems.

"Tony had got this plan together. He had a backer – someone to buy the jewellery. He said the security was crap… I had every confidence in him – there was no way I thought he would betray me, not for two seconds. If this had come to me from someone else – in a pub – I would not have gone along with it, but it was the background to where it had come from. It was solid."

Betson alleged he had developed a trusting relationship with Waring, saying: "I did not think he would try and do me any harm. I trusted him."

When called as a prosecution witness, PC Michael Waring "totally denied" he had been part of the plan or had offered to act in any criminal way by providing information on security at the Dome.

The court heard that the gang had invested tens of thousands of pounds planning the raid and that they stored the equipment they needed at the disused commercial yard in Plumstead, south-east London, as well as those two remote Kent farms near Maidstone. Recently deceased gang member Terry Millman had, the court heard, even used the name "T. Diamond" when he paid £3,700 in cash to purchase the gang's getaway speedboat in Whitstable, Kent.

The court was also told that Ray Betson's criminal career had mainly involved buying goods on the cheap abroad and importing them illegally. Two Customs and Excise raids in late 1999 and early 2000 suddenly left him stockless and broke. He'd been planning to take his family to live in Marbella, but didn't even have enough cash for the plane tickets.

Robert Adams had been a plasterer by trade and his life had been crime-free until he returned from working on a lucrative six-month job in Saudi Arabia to find his best friend had moved into his house with his wife. His friend threatened Adams with a kitchen knife and they fought. As they struggled for possession of the knife, Adams stabbed him in the stomach. He turned himself in and got six years for attempted murder.

Adams made sympathetic new "friends" while inside, and after he got out, he found work as an occasional cash-in-hand plasterer for criminals and did a little cannabis dealing on the side. Betson recruited Adams because he felt Adams deserved a lucky break. Ironically, Adams was said to be a distant relative of Britain's most notorious crime dynasty: the Adams family of north London, who'd amassed a multi-million-pound fortune through drugs.

Betson's best friend, petty thief and builder Bill Cockram, thought the plan was pie in the sky at first, but decided to go along with it when he realized how bad the security at the Dome was.

Ciarrocchi, whose "job" was to stay outside the Dome vault throwing smoke bombs to shield the other robbers – planned to use the £50,000 he was promised for the raid to start a new life in America with his middle-class fiancée, US model Elisabeth Kirsch, 25, who had no idea he was a criminal. Ciarrocchi had pursued her with lavish gifts, including a Cartier watch, before his property-rental business went bust leaving him, like Betson, without enough cash for the airfare to a new life.

Getaway driver Terence Millman, 56, had previous experience of armed robbery and had spent 14 years in prison. He supplied the criminal connections that Betson needed to get the job done, as well as assisting him in creating a foolproof plan. But Millman was on his last legs; this was to be his grand swansong, because he was suffering from terminal cancer of the stomach and lungs. He wanted enough cash to be able to go out with a bang.

Speedboat driver Kevin Meredith, 34, from Brighton, had only one previous offence – for not paying his TV license.

In court, Operation Magician leader, Detective Chief Superintendent Jon Shatford, traced the story of the Dome Raiders back to another audacious robbery attempt in

Britain's Great Train Robbery at Cheddington, Buckinghamshire, 8 August 1963. The train robbers left their army-type truck (where the car is seen) and lugged sacks down to it away from the track. The bridge and underpass are also visible.

The Great Train Robbery, August 1963: the train after the initial police investigation.

An annotated photograph showing how bank robbers tunnelled into the Baker Street branch of Lloyd's Bank in London from an empty shop two doors away. The gang raided 250 safety deposit boxes in the strong room of the bank and escaped with £100,000.

The scene of a robbery at the Baker Street branch of Lloyds Bank, on the corner with Marylebone Road, 13 September 1971. Thieves broke into the vault and made off with thousands of pounds.

London Radio ham enthusiast Robert Rowlands, 32, overheard the bank robbers on his radio and informed the police.

An annotated, overhead view of the vans at Security Express, Shoreditch, London, following the robbery on 5 April 1983.

The doorway of the Security Express offices at Shoreditch, London, following the robbery on 5 April 1983.

Ronnie Knight, pictured in 1980 with his actress wife Barbara Windsor.

The scene outside Unit 7 of the Brink's-Mat security warehouse on the Heathrow Industrial Trading Estate, where armed raiders got away with more than £30 million worth of pure gold. Staff inside were reportedly handcuffed and had petrol poured over them.

Brink's-Mat robber Peter Mitchell, 41.

Brink's-Mat robber John Reed, 37.

Brink's-Mat robber Kenneth Noye, 37.

Undated photo of Valerio Viccei, the Italian mastermind behind one of Britain's biggest robberies, £60 million from Knightsbridge Safe Deposit Centre in London in 1987.

Safety deposit boxes in Knightsbridge, which were robbed in the heist by Valerio Viccei.

Detectives examine rows of deposit boxes, which were smashed open by raiders at the Knightsbridge Safety Deposit Centre in London during Viccei's daring raid.

The notorious JCB digger used in the attempted theft of the
Millennium Dome jewels, 7 November 2000.

CCTV footage of the Millennium Dome robbers attempting to smash
the reinforced glass case protecting the diamonds.

CCTV footage of the white truck (front left), used in the Northern Bank robbery, as it approached the city centre en-route to the bank, 24 December 2004.

A general view of the rear of the Northern Bank in Belfast.

CCTV footage of the robbers holding staff at gunpoint inside the Securitas depot.

CCTV pictures of the well-dressed thieves entering the Graff's jewellery shop on 6 August 2009. The pair got away with 43 jewels and watches. The haul is thought to be the biggest ever netted in the UK, almost doubling the £23m worth of items stolen in a raid on the same shop in 2003.

February 1999, when armed men tried to pull off a £10 million raid on a security van in Nine Elms, south London.

The gunmen had stopped a cash-laden lorry by blocking off both ends of Nine Elms Lane. The plan was to use a lorry carrying Christmas trees nearby as a battering ram. In fact, the foliage camouflaged a huge metal spike welded into the chassis with which the thieves planned to split open the security van's rear doors.

However, an irate motorist who was late for work removed the ignition keys from the unattended Christmas tree van. At a stroke, the robbers' plan had been left in tatters and they fled empty-handed, making their escape in an inflatable speedboat.

"What that day did was to inform me that there was a gang with sufficient organization and capability to carry off a robbery of an intense magnitude," Shatford told the court.

Police tracked some of the vehicles used in that raid to two isolated farms in rural Kent and the properties were immediately put under 24-hour surveillance. By now officers had also received a tip-off about the Dome raid from an informer, whose identity remains a closely guarded secret, but which is thought to be an associate of Brink's-Mat robber and M25 road-rage killer Kenneth Noye.

Two months before the robbery attempt, police saw Betson and Cockram visiting the Dome posing as tourists. At a meeting of detectives hunting the earlier Nine Elms robbers, a detective inspector who'd seen the footage of the two men at the Dome quipped: "Maybe they're after the Millennium jewels?"

"Christ, that's it," cried another. The penny had finally dropped and the police counter-attack was put into action.

More than 100 officers from the Flying Squad were placed on constant standby, backed up by armed officers. But, as Shatford admitted in court: "What I did not know – and I never knew until it happened – was how they were going to do it."

On Monday, 8 February 2002, the Old Bailey jury – consisting of seven women and five men – reached a 10–2 majority verdict against the defendants after deliberating for nearly seven days. Judge Michael Coombe told the robbers: "You played for very high stakes and you must have known perfectly well what the penalty would be if your enterprise did not succeed." The judge added: "This was a wicked, professional plan and one which was carried out with the minutest attention to detail. Mercifully, the police were on to it."

Gang leader Raymond "Black Ray" Betson, now 40, of Chatham, Kent, and his best friend William Cockram, 49, from Catford, south-east London, were each jailed for 18 years. Robert Adams, 57, of no fixed address, and Aldo Ciarrocchi, 32, of Bermondsey, south-east London, each received 15 years. Speedboat driver Kevin Meredith, 34, from Brighton, was cleared of conspiracy to rob, but was convicted of conspiracy to steal and jailed for five years. Another gang member, who sat in a white van monitoring the police radio on the other side of the Thames and who delivered the robbers in a van on the day of the raid, has never been traced.

Another man involved in the robbery plot was jailed at the Old Bailey two days after the main trial had ended. Lee Wenham, 33, was sentenced to four years in jail after pleading guilty to conspiracy to steal. At the same time he was sentenced to nine years after pleading guilty to an attempted robbery that had taken place at Ayelsford, Kent, in June 2000. Wenham had been involved in reconnaissance of the Dome before the raid and had stored the speedboat at his farm in Tonbridge, Kent. In September 2000 he was twice seen in Whitstable harbour testing the speedboat with other conspirators.

After the trial, former Flying Squad chief Shatford, now in charge of the Serious Crime Group in north-east London, said: "I'm delighted with the verdict and sentence. I believe Betson was the mastermind. He is a dangerous man and was known to the Flying Squad. I believe he was responsible for a large number of armed robberies in the past."

While the capture and sentencing of the gang seemed a conspicuous success for the Flying Squad, several awkward questions remained unanswered. Why did the gang believe they could get away with the world's largest theft in broad daylight from what was supposedly Britain's premier tourist attraction? Were they as dangerous as the police made out? And who would want to buy the planet's hottest diamonds? Operation Magician had certainly restored the Flying Squad's tattered reputation after many years of highly publicized corruption scandals, but at what cost?

Betson and Cockram are thought to have stashed away money in offshore bank accounts, but police have never to trace it. All the defendants were on legal aid, landing the taxpayer with a £2 million bill for the three-month trial.

AFTERMATH

Intriguingly, the white van that fled the scene after the robbery attempt was said in court to contain the police's so-called informant or "grass", called Tony, who allegedly set up the job. The white van was traced to the former Old Coal Yard in Plumstead, where the robbery gang had stored their vehicles. In fact, many believe that "Tony" was a name used to distract attention from the *Mr Big* who had bankrolled the raid and who had found a buyer for the diamonds.

That *Mr Big* was Jack Carter (his real name can't be given for legal reasons), one of the most dangerous men in Britain. A middle-aged south Londoner, he rose through the criminal ranks to become one of the most successful drugs traffickers in the world. Despite having his shipments tracked by an RAF Nimrod and an HMS Vanguard submarine in the past, he's always managed to evade arrest.

Tired of the bloody battle for the drugs market, Carter had reverted to financing robberies, which he would safely supervise from a distance. He also became involved in the comparatively risk-free world of VAT fraud. A mutual friend brought Betson into Jack Carter's circle and Betson suggested the Dome job. Ironically, Carter was arrested for VAT fraud in 2000 and several names linked to the Dome job, including Ray Betson and Aldo Ciarrocchi, were found in his address book, which had been confiscated by customs officers. South London underworld insiders claim that Carter is even "looking after" the Dome gang's families following their arrest.

Carter had always assured Betson he'd be able to find

a buyer for the diamonds thanks to his international connections in Marbella – the European Miami, so-called because it attracts drug dealers from all over the world as well as top international criminals. These included gem-smuggler extraordinaire Alexei Vlasov, a lieutenant in the Rising Sun criminal organization. With a network that stretched across Russia, the Middle East and Europe, Vlasov would have had little trouble disposing of the diamond collection. It is alleged that he planned to buy the diamonds for £1 million and would eventually make a net profit on the black market of about £1.5 million to £2 million once they were cut and sold via a large, well-known, seemingly legitimate diamond firm in Antwerp. Carter and the gang would split the £1 million 50-50.

On 24 July 2001, Vlasov was caught smuggling diamonds worth more than £1.5 million after a law-enforcement operation involving the Russian police and the CIA. Viasov was also charged with 13 other black-market diamond deals and is now serving time in a Russian jail. On his Interpol red notice (an arrest warrant detailing a criminal's activities), an associate of Jack Carter's is listed as one of Viasov's main accomplices.

The police operation to catch the Dome Raiders cost £3.5 million, including the cost of the Old Bailey trial. In return, the Flying Squad removed a handful of criminals off the streets of London for a dozen or so years. But *Mr Big*, Jack Carter, continues to make millions out of Britain's underworld. He is also thought to have been involved in financing a number of other gold and cash robberies. According to word on the streets of south London, the Dome Raiders themselves feel hard done by, but as Great Train Robber Ronnie Biggs said to gang member Bill Cockram when he found out what he was in for: *"Bloody 'ell, we never learn, do we?"*

The failure of the Dome Heist sparked new, disturbing developments in the UK underworld. Teams of robbers began emerging whose targets were not banks or jewellers or money warehouses. They were well organized, cold and cunning – and they were after top-of-the-range cars. It was a radical difference from the traditional "good old days" when blaggers would charge across a pavement brandishing sawn-offs for a bag of cash.

During the first couple of years of the new millennium, "carjackings" were in fashion. Stolen luxury vehicles – especially 4x4s – had a roaring market all over the rest of Europe and the Middle East as well as in certain parts of Africa, and gangs of robbers began to steal to order.

In 2001, 25-year-old estate agent Tim Robinson was stabbed to death in south London in front of his fiancée as he parked his car outside his home. His two teenage assailants were only after his £30,000 Audi. There is absolutely no doubt they were working on behalf of a gang of professional car "handlers" who would ship the car abroad within hours of the theft.

A few days later, in Dulwich, south London, a woman was violently pushed out of her BMW sports car at night. In another incident, a mother got out of her £45,000 four-wheel drive car to drop off a letter, only to turn and see two blaggers driving away in her car with her screaming children inside.

The children were released a short distance away, but neither the car nor the offenders were ever traced.

Police came down heavily on the carjacking gangs, thanks to CCTV cameras, sophisticated in-car tracking devices and DNA. But, more importantly, as one old-time blagger explained many years later: "Carjacking was a bloody liberty. The cozzers had to come down hard on these robbers because they'd stepped across the line. Nicking out of a bank or a security van is all very well, but threatening people in their cars is completely out of order."

So after a flurry of dramatic carjacking arrests, the villains turned back their attention to more traditional targets. And they didn't come more obvious and more lucrative than Heathrow Airport.

9. WEAK SPOT

"People seem to be glorifying the offence of armed robbery and I can only reiterate that I hope the sentences the courts have imposed today will send out a clear message."

Detective Superintendent Barry Phillips

Heathrow Airport, London, Monday, 11 February 2002, 6.30am

Part-time van driver Sundeep Sidhu, 22, had been given special permission to help collect a consignment arriving on BA Flight 124 due to the overstretched staffing situation at the airport. The flight had left Bahrain at 2am local time that morning and was due at Heathrow at 6.45am. In fact, the Boeing 777 touched down early, just after 6am, and taxied to a stand 300 metres from the main Terminal Four building. The plane was due to refuel before flying on to New York's JFK Airport.

So, along with his supervisor, Sidhu arrived next to the plane airside in his airport security van. Two silver cash boxes were unloaded from the plane straight into the vehicle. Those boxes were to be taken directly to a secure area near Terminal Four before being put back on the plane just before its eventual departure for the US.

The supervisor left the plane moments before the two cash boxes were unloaded in the terminal's secure area. As he was walking towards the main terminal building, he was stunned when the van suddenly drove off at high speed towards the Gate 25 exit from the airport perimeter.

Driver Sidhu – a £200-a-week part-timer – later recalled two Asian males had appeared from nowhere in the back of the vehicle, threatened him with knives and told him to drive the vehicle out of the airport. Sidhu's van was waved through Gate 25 by security guards moments after it was driven away from that secure area. The vehicle then headed at speed along Stanwell Road alongside the airport perimeter before crossing the main A30 road and turning into Spinney Drive, in the district of Feltham, a couple of miles from Heathrow.

Driver Sidhu was then forced out of the van by the two robbers, who threw him to the ground and tied his hands behind his back before transferring the cash boxes from the BA vehicle into a waiting Renault Mastervan, also with BA markings. It was actually a stolen transfer-baggage van.

After completing the transfer of the cash, the robbers left Sidhu on the ground and fled in the stolen van

A police helicopter later searching the area around Heathrow and Feltham for the gang found the blaggers' burnt-out BA van dumped on wasteground. There was no sign of the cash. Detectives assumed either accomplices had picked up the robbers or that they had jumped into another vehicle parked nearby.

Minutes after the initial heist, airport police – alerted by Sidhu's shocked supervisor – found the airport driver sprawled on the ground next to his own van, his wrists bound. Shaken and with minor injuries, Sidhu said at least two men had attacked him but that he had not seen any firearms on them. Sidhu was taken to hospital, where he was treated for shock and cuts to his wrists, but doctors said his condition was not serious.

Within minutes of arriving at the cargo terminal's safe area, police began interviewing security staff and officials to try and find out exactly how the thieves got into the secure area and ambushed the van driver. Detectives described it as a slick and simple heist. One said: "There are hundreds of BA vans driving around Heathrow at any time. There was no reason for them to be stopped. The whole operation was over in minutes. These were professionals."

The fact that a robbery could take place in a secure airside area at Heathrow immediately raised security concerns. Asked how the robbers could have gained access, one detective admitted: "That may be the key to solving this crime."

Scotland Yard's robbery experts, the Flying Squad, were soon on the scene. They were just as alarmed by how the gang had managed to enter the secure area and also wondered how they knew the money was on the flight.

Was this a daring, simple, superbly executed raid by some "old hands"? Or was it an inside job, executed by a bunch of opportunistic villains? Surely authorities would have noticed any earlier reconnaissance trips by the gang inside the airport perimeter? With all airports on high alert since the 11 September 2001, terrorist attacks, police presumed any unusual activity in the days before the robbery would have been noticed.

In fact, the raid had followed a series of security lapses at British airports, all of which had taken place – despite the extra security measures in place since 11 September. Tactfully, the Flying Squad refused to say if the incident had prompted a new review of security at Heathrow, but admitted: "Security is always under review."

Privately, many in government were furious that such a daring robbery had happened in what was supposed to be one of the most secure airports in the world. But the police soon started to suspect that this job was nothing to do with a lapse in security, rather that the thieves must have been insiders who knew exactly when the BA driver was due to pick up the cash.

Intriguingly, the reason for moving such a large amount of money on a scheduled flight has never been properly disclosed. Bahrain is one of the most important banking centres in the Middle East, but it was unlikely an institution would transfer the cash on such a flight. For the moment, however, the police's top priority was to catch the blaggers rather than question the circumstances as to why the cash was in transit in the first place.

Even the British Airports Authority openly admitted the robbers must have had legitimate passes to gain access to the security-controlled zone. Airport officials also concluded that the gang must have had a detailed knowledge of security procedures, as well as of the best and fastest routes in and around Heathrow.

The aviation security editor of *Jane's Defence Weekly*, Chris Yates, described the heist as one of the most serious breaches of security at any British airport. "If anyone can simply drive through the perimeter, and particularly at a major airport like Heathrow, then their ought to be some serious questions asked about how we go about security here in the UK," he told the BBC.

Meanwhile, detectives were closely studying CCTV footage from the secure area in the hope it might provide some clues about the robbery. They'd already put together descriptions of the two robbers. They were described as Asian. One, thought to be the driver of the stolen van, was in his 20s to 30s, 5 feet 11 inches tall and of slim build. He was wearing a green khaki jacket, sunglasses and a coloured bobble hat. He had long hair. The second suspect was aged in his early 40s and of medium to stocky build. He was clean-shaven, balding with short hair and was wearing a high- visibility BA jacket.

After circulating the descriptions, the Flying Squad issued a public appeal for witnesses who may have seen the robbers escaping from the airport after the robbery. Detectives knew the men had left through Gate 25 at the airport in the British Airways security van and wondered why the vehicle was allowed to get through the security checks so easily.

The following morning, one newspaper report summed up the heist and its aftermath: *Robbers yesterday fled with £4.6 million in a meticulously planned heist at Heathrow, embarrassing both the airport authorities and British Airways, which had brought in tougher security measures after 11 September.*

Not surprisingly, long-in-the-tooth Flying Squad detectives were far from convinced by van driver Sundeep Sidhu's story and decided to mount a special surveillance operation targeting both him and his brother Harjit, 25.

For two months, detectives secretly filmed the brothers and a number of their associates. They even brought in a specialist lip-reader to transcribe their surveillance footage. Evidence from that lip-reader proved crucial, because Harjit Sidhu was filmed by detectives bragging about how he was "going to Hawaii later in the year" and that police "haven't sussed anything". An associate of the two brothers was then filmed telling another man: "Everybody will get £250,000. We have got it, it is all over the place."

- Sidhu was seen with brother Harjit – who detectives now believed was a leading member of the gang – talking animatedly on a park bench near their home in Uxbridge, Middlesex. The brothers were then seen meeting associates Anil Parmar, 37, of Northolt, Manish Bhadresa, 23, of Southall and Harbhajan Padda, 33, of Isleworth. Detectives soon concluded they were all members of the robbery gang.

- Harjit Sidhu was then secretly filmed sitting with fellow suspect Padda in a car parked at the end of a cul-de-sac in Hounslow. Sidhu told Padda he was going to buy a house in upmarket Weybridge, Surrey. Harjit said to Padda: "No one suspected… the police have not sussed anything."

- Harjit went on to say he'd deny everything if the police ever quizzed him. "They've got no evidence," he bragged, totally unaware that undercover officers were filming him from a safe distance at that very moment.

- Harjit added: "If the police think it's me, I just say, 'So then, where's the money?' They won't have a thing on us."

- At a meeting outside a pub in Southall, Middlesex, Harjit and his friend Parmar discussed how they were going to change their stolen dollars into sterling without arousing suspicion. Then, at a McDonald's burger bar in Southall, the suspects were again filmed talking in English about their crime.

Police even mingled with worshippers at an Indian religious festival in Southall and filmed the gang talking again about the heist and discussing more details about how to change currency.

The police lip-reader even managed to transcribe what gang members were saying while they spoke on mobile phones.

One detective on the case later described the lip-reader as "our secret weapon". He said: "The evidence from the lip-reader was quite incredible. She pointed us in the right direction and was able to give us cast-iron evidence about the crime. Even if they had suspected a tail, they would never have dreamed anyone would be able to work out what they were saying. There were no electronic devices, it was just old-fashioned lip-reading."

The brothers and the three other members of the gang eventually confessed to the robbery after the Flying Squad executed dawn raids on addresses in west London. Cash found at gang member Manish Bhadresa's home in Southall included £81,000, $297,000, 93,000 euros, 260 Irish punts and 117,000 Kenyan shillings. The gang had even thrown away thousands of pounds worth of cash in currencies they did not recognize.

At the gang's eventual trial at Kingston Crown Court, Sundeep Sidhu, of St Mary's Avenue, Norwood Green, west London, pleaded guilty to theft and was sentenced to five-and-a-half years in prison for the "grave breach of trust" he inflicted on his company, ADI Securicor.

His brother Harjit Sidhu, also of St Mary's Avenue, Anil Parmar, of De Havilland Close, Northolt, west London, and Manish Bhadresa, of Trinity Road, Southall, west London, all pleaded guilty to theft and were jailed for five years. Harbhajan Padda, of London Road, Isleworth, south-west London was jailed for five years after pleading guilty to handling stolen goods.

But, months earlier, while police were filming the suspects before their arrest, another gang of Asian robbers were about to try and pull off a copycat job at Heathrow airport…

THE COPYCAT JOB

This time the robbers swooped on a Securicor van, also inside the Heathrow Airport perimeter, at 7am on 13 March, just six weeks after the first Heathrow job. They watched and waited for the perfect moment to swoop as airline passengers were taken to the terminal in a bus while their luggage – and $6.5 million in eight red cargo cashboxes – was unloaded. The money was due to be transferred into a BA van and then delivered to another flight due to leave for New York's JFK airport. *No wonder many in the UK underworld refer to Heathrow as "Thiefrow".*

The 35-year-old driver of the van later told police that he was sitting in the driver's seat when the two suspects approached him and ordered him to drive from the airport to Church Road, Cranford, where the cashboxes were transferred into another vehicle.

UK government ministers immediately demanded an inquiry into what had been yet another security lapse at Heathrow Airport; it was, after all, the second multi-million pound heist at the airport in just five weeks. There were genuine fears that the airport could be at risk of a terrorist attack if it was so easy to carry out such robberies.

Detectives, meanwhile, officially kept an "open mind" about any links between the two heists, because they didn't want to admit publicly they were already many weeks into the surveillance operation on the first robbery gang.

Police later arrested 12 people and recovered a "substantial amount of money" in connection with the second robbery.

Following the sentencing of the gang responsible for the

second raid, Detective Superintendent Barry Phillips said: "People seem to be glorifying the offence of armed robbery and I can only reiterate that I hope the sentences the courts have imposed today will send out a clear message."

AFTERMATH

Amazingly, despite the police successes with regard to these two major Heathrow jobs, blaggers continued to regard the UK's main airport as a prime robbery target.

In May 2004, a white Transit van containing a gang of robbers rammed through the shutters of the Swiss Port Cargo warehouse on the outer perimeter of Heathrow. The bandits emerged brandishing firearms and other weapons, including knives and cudgels. They were after a large quantity of precious metal – including gold bullion and banknotes worth a total of £40 million – which had just been delivered to the warehouse. An inside man had given them the nod and they believed they were on the verge of underworld notoriety.

But within seconds of the raid, Flying Squad officers – backed up by a team from the Met's specialist SO19 firearms unit – fired baton rounds at the van and instantly disabled it. Six men were arrested, while two others escaped after hijacking another van and forcing the driver to take them out of the airport towards Stanwell, west London. The van and its entirely innocent driver were later safely recovered. The Met operation, codenamed "Cartwright", had successfully thwarted a gang of robbers who would have ended up with a bigger haul than the notorious Brink's-Mat job if they had succeeded.

But as one veteran robber told me very recently: "Heathrow was once paved in gold, literally, but these days it's a definite no-no. Security cameras and the fact they've completely tightened up all the perimeter controls mean only a fool would try and pull off a major blagging there these days."

Give it time…

10. WHO PLAYED THE TUNE?

"The IRA has been accused of involvement in the recent Northern Bank robbery. We were not involved."

Provisional IRA's two-line statement issued on 18 January 2005

Northern Bank, outskirts of Belfast, Northern Ireland,
Sunday, 19 December 2004, 10pm

It was a bitterly cold Sunday night. Christmas was around the corner and most people were just happy to be safely tucked up in their homes.

But two innocent families were about to be targeted by one of the most daring, and successful, robbery gangs of all time. None of the blaggers was ever brought to justice and their job almost single-handedly set the Northern Ireland Peace Process back years.

Despite consistent denials, the heist had all the hallmarks of the work of a well-organized terrorist organization, even down to the way the gang used two groups of armed men to call at the homes of two officials of the Donegall Square West branch of the province's Northern Bank and "persuade" them to co-operate.

One lived in Downpatrick, County Down, the other in Poleglass, near Belfast. Masquerading as police officers, members of the robbery gang entered both homes simultaneously before pulling out guns and holding workers' families under a 24-hour "armed guard".

When bank worker Chris Ward arrived at his Poleglass home, two masked men had already taken his parents, brother and his girlfriend hostage. In virtually an identical raid, Ward's Northern Bank supervisor, Kevin McMullan, and his wife Karen had been tied up at gunpoint by two other masked men.

Ward identified himself to the robbers and was ordered out of his home at gunpoint to a waiting red car, which then took him to McMullan's house. Both bank workers knew exactly what the gang's intentions were the moment Ward was shoved through the front door of his boss's house.

At 11.30pm – following some kind of incident that has never been publicly revealed – McMullan's wife Karen was dragged out of the house and thrown into the back of the same red car and then taken blindfolded to an undisclosed location, where she would be held for more than 24 hours.

Back at McMullan's home, the gang ordered both bank officials to go to work as usual the following day at their offices beside Belfast City Hall. They were told to go through their normal routine, chatting to colleagues as if nothing unusual had happened. The robbers knew the two bank officials worked in the cash centre in the bank's basement and they also knew that it would be overflowing with cash in the run-up to Christmas.

One of the gang even patiently explained to Ward that he'd be put to a special "test" to make sure the robbery went smoothly. Ward was told to steal £1 million from the bank during opening hours and to take it in a holdall to one of the gang, who'd be waiting near the branch office. It was a very unusual move, but as one old-time robber told me years later: "It was a smart move. I wish I'd thought of something like that meself."

Ward himself didn't dare ask why he was being asked to steal £1 million *before* the gang committed the main heist. He just gulped and slowly nodded his head in reluctant agreement when he was told what was expected of him.

The masked men also gave Ward and McMullan further, detailed instructions as to what they specifically needed to do inside the bank, with the omnipresent threat of death for their innocent family members hanging over their heads if they didn't comply. The gang stated their orders with military precision, which made them an even more frightening force for the two bank workers to deal with. Finally, Ward was told where he should drop the £1 million cash the following lunchtime. Both men later said that they had no doubt they and their families would be killed if they didn't stick exactly to the letter of what the gang were expecting.

The following morning – Monday, 20 December 2004 – Ward and McMullan went to work hiding a huge, cruel secret that they couldn't reveal to anyone. Both of them were terrified that if they put a foot wrong their loved ones would pay for it with their lives. But somehow the two men managed to carry out their normal daily duties as if nothing was wrong. Occasionally, they would glance at each other nervously as the day progressed, but not once did either of them mention the awful events of the previous evening to anyone else, not even to each other.

At lunchtime, Ward was able to remove the cash under the pretext that a customer was coming in that afternoon to make a withdrawal. He then discretely placed the cash in the sports holdall the gang had given him the previous evening. Some time later, Ward told his fellow workers he was popping out for a sandwich and strolled out of the bank's Wellington Street staff entrance with the bag containing the money.

Ward made his way slowly and nervously alongside the pavement close to the perimeter of the bank, trying hard not to catch the eye of any passing pedestrians. On at least two occasions, Ward glanced behind him to see if anyone was following him. Then, as instructed by the gang, he reached a bus-stop in nearby Queen Street, but no one was there as a bus had just driven off. Thrown by this, Ward walked around the block once again rather than stand awkwardly at the bus-stop. When he returned, a man wearing a baseball cap was waiting for him.

Without exchanging a word, Ward handed the holdall containing £1 million cash to the man and he walked off. CCTV footage later recovered by police clearly showed Ward's movements.

Ward could barely walk straight as he made his way back to the bank. His legs were like jelly and he was confused because he'd just been forced to commit a crime, but he felt as if he was now implicated in the robbery. Worse still, he didn't have a person in the world he could turn to. It was an awful predicament. As he said many years later: "I felt like the loneliest person in the world at that moment."

But, somehow, Ward managed to go back to work inside the bank without anyone noticing his nervous disposition. For the following five hours he kept up this pretence, occasionally explaining his quietness to other workers by saying he thought he might be coming down with the flu.

Many later speculated that Ward's "chore" in stealing that £1 million cash was a test run for the main robbery later that evening. In fact, one old-time blagger told me he reckoned it was a lot more than just that: "It was a brilliant move on the part of the blaggers, because not only did it ensure that the bank worker was now incriminated in the robbery, but it also guaranteed to the gang that if all else went wrong they had a million quid tucked away somewhere for a rainy day. What superb operators. Amazing!"

No one can actually go inside the heads of those two bank officials, but it's hard not to presume they were feeling completely overawed by the pressure they were under. One robbery victim who went through a similar experience once told me: "It's a horrible feeling. There is nowhere to turn, literally. Those two men must have felt as if they were in a living nightmare and they had no idea how it was all going to end."

By the time all the other bank employees had gone home at 6pm, both men must have felt a bizarre sense of relief, because now they only had to deal with the robbers. Ward and McMullan were key-holders, so they were quickly able to let the gang into the building via the Wellington Street staff entrance.

The two bank workers then led the blaggers to the basement, which housed the bank's cash-handling and storage facility. As the robbers already knew, it contained that unusually large amount of cash in preparation for distribution to automated teller machines for the busy Christmas shopping season.

The gang then began packing the cash into black plastic rubbish bags as the two bank employees stood "on duty" outside the vault, in case either of the bank's two security guards appeared. Amazingly, there were no specific CCTV cameras pointed at the area where the cash was actually being stolen from.

At 7pm, a scruffy white van pulled up outside the Wellington Street exit of the bank. The gang quickly began loading rubbish bags filled with cash into the back of the vehicle.

McMullan later recounted how, during the actual robbery, he was standing in the bank's bullion loading bay with two trolleys filled with rubbish bags containing millions in notes when one of the bank's security guards wandered over for a chat, completely unaware that a robbery was in progress. "I was going to have to be the boss. I was going to have to be a fantastic actor," he later explained.

The two men watched as the robbers loaded the van with what McMullan casually told the guard "bags of rubbish".

The guard eventually left the loading bay none the wiser. McMullan later explained that he was prepared to do anything to ensure the safety of his family. They were his only priority.

A few minutes later, the scruffy white "rubbish" van departed and drove off in the direction of the nearby Grosvenor Road roundabout. It would return less than 15 minutes later for a second load of cash.

At around 8.10pm, a man and a woman, who were shopping in the area, saw two men, who seemed to be wearing wigs, acting suspiciously and hanging around a white van parked at the side of the bank. Three minutes later, the couple reported the incident to a traffic warden, who passed the information on to the police. Two constables patrolling the area were alerted and arrived at the bank at 8.18pm, narrowly missing the gang, who had driven off for the second and last cash collection. The constables reported nothing amiss and continued their patrol.

With uninterrupted access to the vaults, the gang had managed to pack as much cash as possible into their vehicle. The total haul would consist of £26.5 million in cash, mostly un-circulated Northern Bank notes, but also included £8.85 million sterling in used notes, and over a million pounds in other currencies such as US dollars and euros. As it was, the size of the haul may even have taken the gang by surprise.

The full details of what happened after the van's last cash collection have never been revealed. However, it seems that both bank workers – mindful that if they put a foot wrong their families could still be killed – obeyed the gang's orders and simply left the bank and headed back to their homes.

The two bank employers faced a terrifying dilemma: they knew they couldn't raise the alarm because, if they did, it could risk the lives of their families. They would have to wait until the blaggers decided it was safe to release the family members.

Shortly before midnight, suffering from exposure due to the extreme cold and in a state of shock after being released by her captors in the middle of Drumkeeragh Forest Park, County Down, McMullan's wife Karen found her way to a house to raise the alarm. Her burnt-out car was later found in the Forest Park.

At the Ward family home nearer to Belfast, armed men holding the family had left the property around the same time that their associates were releasing Mrs McMullan. At last the ordeal for these two innocent families was over.

Within minutes of the release of the family members, police and senior Northern Bank officials were alerted to the robbery. Head of Northern Ireland's Crime Operations branch, Sam Kincaid, was briefed and immediately launched a hunt for the gang.

But the robbery and its ancillary "work" with the two families had been so carefully orchestrated and executed that many valuable hours had passed since the bank had been robbed, giving the blaggers a lot of time to disperse. The Belfast blagging brings gasps of admiration from the criminal fraternity, even to this day.

One old blagger told me recently: "This is the one that stands out above all other robberies. These guys thought of everything. They were one step ahead of the police throughout. It's not surprising they got away with it."

Belfast was stunned when news of the heist began spreading through the city. Politicians on both sides of the religious divide immediately began pointing the finger of suspicion at terrorist groups. No one could quite believe that maybe it was simply a brilliantly carried out crime that was committed purely for cash.

Typical of the tinderbox political scene in Northern Ireland, this audacious robbery threatened huge political ramifications for the province's peace process, coming at a particularly delicate time in the negotiations.

Meanwhile, Northern Bank announced that it would recall all £300 million worth of its banknotes in denominations of £10 or more, and reissue them in different colours with both new logos and serial numbers. The first of these new notes would enter circulation within six weeks.

But few believed the bank's response would prevent the robbers cashing in at least some of the stolen notes before they were reissued. One south London blagger told me he'd heard that the notes were spread around the province within days and weeks of the raid and had been exchanged for "untarnished" currency in numerous, perfectly innocent cash transactions. If that is the case, then it seems the robbers may well have made at least 50 per cent of their total haul before the reissue of the notes by the bank.

Back on the redhot Belfast political scene, prominent Northern Ireland commentators pointed the finger at the Provisional IRA, saying that only it had the wherewithal to pull off such a professional operation in the province. One senior police officer was even quoted in the *Guardian* newspaper saying: "This operation required great expertise and co-ordination, probably more than the loyalist gangs possess."

Two weeks after the robbery, Hugh Orde, the province's Chief Constable, issued an interim report in which he blamed the Provisional IRA for the Belfast job. The British and Irish governments concurred with Orde's assessment, as did the

Independent Monitoring Commission (the body appointed by the Irish and British governments to oversee the Northern Ireland ceasefire).

The political wing of the IRA, Sinn Féin, however, denied the Chief Constable's claim, saying the IRA had no connection to the raid and that Sinn Féin officials had not known about or sanctioned the robbery. Sinn Féin's Martin McGuinness said that Orde's accusation represented "nothing more than politically-biased allegations... This is more to do with halting the process of change which Sinn Féin has been driving forward than with anything that happened at the Northern Bank."

The Provisional IRA even issued a terse two-line public statement denying any connection to the robbery: *The IRA has been accused of involvement in the recent Northern Bank robbery. We were not involved.*

But many remained convinced that that IRA intended to use the cash to secure a pension fund for its active service members, who'd been largely unemployed since the Good Friday Agreement. It was a twisted theory since by "pensioning off" any active terrorists it would probably help the peace process in the province in the long term.

The police made seven arrests in the two months following the heist. One of those detained was a member of Sinn Féin. Another was bank worker Chris Ward, whom the police alleged was the gang's "inside man", but they were all eventually released.

Police did recover £2 million – including £60,000 of Northern Bank notes – during raids in Cork and Dublin. And around $100,000 in US banknotes was found in the toilet of the Police Athletics Association's Newforge Country Club. The Police Service of Northern Ireland confirmed the money was taken during the Northern Bank heist, but said the stash was likely to have been "planted to distract detectives" investigating the robbery and "divert attention from events elsewhere".

It seemed the gang were still "playing games" with the police. This was one heist where the bad guys were winning hands down. Many in Northern Ireland presume the Northern Bank robbery will never be solved and, to date, they have been proved entirely correct.

It wasn't until three years after the heist that bank worker Chris Ward was publicly and fully acquitted of all suspicion that he was the gang's inside man. Ward had maintained his innocence throughout and, eventually, the office of the Director for Public Prosecutions admitted they could not present any concrete evidence against him. He was acquitted and found innocent of all accusations.

Ward's solicitor, Niall Murphy, said afterwards: "Chris Ward is relieved that today his innocence, which he has resolutely maintained since he was first charged almost three years ago, has finally been vindicated in a manner which is surely unique in the history of our legal system. The whole experience for himself and his family, who were victims of kidnapping, false imprisonment and robbery, was truly devastating."

Murphy added: "This has been utterly compounded by his arrest, his detention for the longest period of any individual ever held in police custody in this jurisdiction, and being put on trial for a crime he did not commit and his life thereby destroyed."

AFTERMATH

Only three were ever charged in connection with the Northern Bank robbery. However, to the frustration of detectives, no one has ever been nailed for actually carrying out the heist. To this day, the robbers themselves remain unknown, making it one of the most "perfect jobs" in criminal history.

11. TIGER ATTACK

"Don't do anything silly – we know where you live."

One of the robbers to staff at depot.

Securitas Depot, Tonbridge, Kent, 21 February 2006, 5.30pm

Just before manager Colin Dixon swept out of the depot in his Nissan Almera to begin his 50-mile journey home, he texted his wife to tell her he was on the way home, as he always did most evenings after work. Less than an hour later, as he drove on the A249 between Maidstone and Sittingbourne, Dixon noticed the flashing blue light of a Volvo police car in his rear-view mirror.

Dixon was puzzled, because he always stuck rigidly to the speed limit. Maybe it was a routine check? So, like any law-abiding citizen, he reacted to the police car's flashing lights and pulled over in a lay-by on the busy main road.

The two officers seemed friendly enough at first. Even when

one of them said Dixon had been recorded driving at over the speed limit a few minutes earlier, Dixon accepted their word. But when the two policemen suggested Dixon sit in the back of their patrol car while they checked out his licence-plate details, he became more suspicious. When the two officers noticed his reticence, they virtually bundled Dixon into their vehicle and handcuffed him. He was outraged and confused by what he perceived to be their complete "overreaction".

Dixon was even more bewildered when he heard *BBC Radio One* playing on the car stereo instead of a police channel. As the patrol car moved off hurriedly in the direction of Tonbridge, Dixon demanded to see the policemen's identifications. He was told their cards were "back at the station".

Then one of the officers turned to Dixon and said: "We're not policemen. Don't do anything silly and you won't get hurt."

The officer in the passenger seat then pulled out a gun and pointed it directly at Dixon: "We're not fuckin' about – this is a 9mm."

Dixon was shocked, but managed to remain calm. In the back of his mind, he'd always known that, because of his job, there was a possibility something like this might happen.

Minutes later the police car screeched to a halt by the side of the road and Dixon was pulled out by the two men. He was then pushed towards the back doors of a waiting white van. When Dixon resisted he was told to get in if he didn't want to "get a hole" in him. Once inside, Dixon's legs and hands were bound and his eyes were covered with sticky tape.

Back home in Herne Bay, Dixon's wife, Lynn, was finding it

difficult to concentrate on watching TV because her husband still hadn't arrived home. Lynn had been made well aware of the risks connected to Colin's job before he even began work at Securitas seven years earlier. After all, the depot was used to store millions of pounds in banknotes before they were redistributed to banks and cash machines.

The couple even made a point of swapping cars on a weekly basis and varied their routes to and from work. These measures were taken as a safety precaution, nothing more. However, the longer she waited for her husband, the more doubt went through her head. When she rang her husband's mobile, she was greeted by her husband's answer-phone message. It was odd – Colin *always* picked up the phone. She called the number again, but with the same result.

Nearly 50 miles away, Colin Dixon remained in the back of that white van. He was aware that the men were waiting for something, but he never guessed what it might be. Minutes later, the van stopped in a lay-by.

"Nearly time for a chat, Colin," said one of the men sitting next to him in the back of the van. He felt the barrel of a gun pushed into his ribs. "We'll be needing to know all about the layout at the depot."

Then, eerily, the men said nothing more. It left Colin Dixon fearing for the worst.

Back in Herne Bay, Lynn Dixon had decided that if she didn't hear from her husband by 10pm, she was going to call the police. Then, at 9.45pm, came a knock at the door. Lynn took a long, deep breath. She feared the worse when she looked through the window and saw two policemen standing on her doorstep.

Within moments of opening her front door, Lynn was told that her husband had been in an accident and that she should come with them to the hospital. They suggested she should bring her child with her and stood in the child's room while she got a bag ready.

As Lynn headed with her child to the waiting police car, she began to have serious doubts about the validity of the "police officers", but she pushed those thoughts to the back of her head for the moment, dismissing them as an overreaction. Once she was inside the car, however, Lynn's suspicions were raised again because, just like her husband earlier, she noticed that the radio was not on the police channel. Alarm bells now began to ring very loudly in her head.

Lynn Dixon demanded the policemen show her proof of their identification. She was told gruffly by one of them that it was "in the boot". The way the driver then glanced at his companion increased her anxiety. That's when she screamed. One of the men instantly shoved his black leather gloved hand across her mouth as her child started to cry.

"Shut the fuck up. We've got guns and we'll use 'em if we 'ave to," said one of the men.

Lynn and her child now faced men dressed entirely in black, whose faces and heads were covered by masks with slits for eyes and mouths, brandishing deadly weapons and yelling: "You will die if you do not do as you're told."

Less than an hour later, Lynn and her child were bundled into the same van her husband had been thrown into earlier. They were forced to kneel while guns were pointed at their heads.

A phone was then brought to her mouth and she was

ordered to say something to her husband, so that he would realize his wife and young child had also been snatched. Colin Dixon's heart sank when he heard their voices.

The van containing the Dixons and their armed captors eventually arrived at an isolated £1.5-million mock-Tudor manor house called Elderden Farm, near the Kent village of Staplehurst.

Colin Dixon had the tape removed from his eyes and he was shown a map of the Securitas depot where he worked. He was told to co-operate; if not, his wife and child would be harmed. Not surprisingly, Dixon told the men everything they wanted to know.

Police later dubbed the raid a "tiger kidnapping", so called because of its predatory nature, in which a man and his family were held hostage to force him to comply with their demands.

Just after midnight, Colin Dixon, his wife and child were bundled back into the white van, which was part of a convoy that set off from Elderden farm. All three Dixon family members remained behind under the armed guard of two of the criminal gang. The convoy consisted of the "police" Volvo in the lead, a 7.5-ton Renault lorry, the white van and a Vauxhall Vectra. They drove straight to the Securitas depot in Tonbridge, 20 miles away.

The six-man gang – armed with handguns, shotguns, a *Skorpion* gun and AK-47s – pulled their "priority" captive Colin Dixon out of the van when they arrived at the bunker-style depot. The time was 1.28am.

Dixon, accompanied by one of the gang still disguised as a policeman, used his swipe card to gain entry. It later emerged that all the gang were wearing prosthetics, as used in film and theatre, to change their appearances. The kidnappers believed this would make them unrecognizable and impossible to identify at a later stage.

After swiping his entry card, Dixon and the "policeman" swept through an entrance in the depot's high-steel fence perimeter. Gary Barclay, the Securitas staff member on duty in the control room that morning, saw what he at first thought was his boss and a policeman approaching. But then, as he opened the door to them, Dixon told him: "Just do whatever this bloke says."

Barclay immediately did what he was told. Perhaps he was mindful of the poster on a nearby wall advising staff: *Don't be a hero*. The gang tied up Barclay while Dixon pressed the relevant switches to enable the convoy of three vehicles to drive into the depot compound.

At first, some staff members failed to recognize the seriousness of the situation; night supervisor Melanie Sampson believed Dixon and the "policeman" were part of a training exercise, until she and her colleagues were told by the "officer" to raise their hands and lie on the floor. The robbers tied her hands so tightly that she would lose circulation in them.

The raiders, seen in CCTV footage wearing balaclavas and brandishing their fearsome collection of weapons, threatened to kill staff members if they did not co-operate. One raider even raced maniacally into the ladies' toilets to confront a staff member who was in there, forcing her roughly to the ground at gunpoint, causing her mouth to bleed.

Still carrying their guns, the gang then rapidly moved further into the building and took control of the remaining Securitas staff, handcuffing them and making them lie on the floor. Then they used a forklift truck and a shopping trolley to begin moving cages full of cash into their getaway truck, which was now parked in the loading bay.

Despite their elaborate disguises, witnesses later identified two of the robbers who were disguised as policemen. Further CCTV footage caught one of them orchestrating the heist. Using a timepiece around his neck, he counted down the minutes out loud to his "team". Police later nicknamed him "Stopwatch". Footage also showed the same robber clambering over cash cages as the robbers emptied them.

Then Colin Dixon's wife Lynn and his child were bundled from a van into the vault alongside the tied-up staff. They were then all locked in empty cages and warned: "You will die if you do not do as you are told."

The entire raid had taken one hour and six minutes. By robbery standards it was a luxurious schedule, but then the team knew exactly what they were doing. Each had his own duty to perform. As the robbers left, they told staff: "Don't do anything silly – we know where you live."

Staff member Melanie Sampson later recalled how she only realized the robbery was over when she heard one gang member shout: "Come on, let's rock and roll!" Another raider even thanked the workers sarcastically for their "co-operation" as they departed the scene.

The gang had arrived at 1.28am and left at 2.43am. In just 75 minutes they had taken £52,996,760 in cash, but left behind another £153,833,020.73, purely because they had all agreed in advance not to stay on the premises for any longer than a set amount of time.

The staff, along with Colin Dixon's wife and son, remained locked in those cash cages for another half an hour. However, one member of staff had a key to unlock the cage. She was able to pass it through a tiny gap in the cage to the Dixon's child who was then able to start freeing the workforce. Dixon then raised the alarm. Other staff members hailed his young child a hero.

Police arriving at the scene of the robbery were stunned by the size of the robbers' haul and recognized that it was probably going to turn out to be the biggest cash robbery in British criminal history. The Bank of England initially admitted more than £25 million had been stolen, but later reports more than doubled that figure and the authorities have never since denied it.

Detectives were convinced the gang must have known in advance that February was the month when the greatest amount of cash is taken out of circulation in Britain and held briefly in storage. It was the prime time for a gang of robbers to strike. One detective at the scene told reporters: "These blaggers were real pros, but they had to have some inside help to pull this one off."

In fact the robbers did have that other "weapon" in their arsenal: inside man Ermir Hysenaj, a 28-year-old Albanian, who'd recently started work at Securitas. He became the gang's eyes and ears in the weeks before the robbery. He scouted the premises, filmed the layout and security precautions and gave them invaluable "help".

Hours after the robbery, Detective Superintendent Paul Gladstone of Kent Police told reporters the victims were "all coping extremely well considering the circumstances. They were threatened with extreme violence by the gang and underwent a terrifying ordeal. This gang were highly sophisticated and organized. They are not amateurs. This was a clearly a robbery that was planned in detail over time."

Police also began checking closed-circuit television footage from the nearby Channel Tunnel in Kent to see if the gang had fled to France. Others wondered if the blaggers had "done a Brink's-Mat" and had no idea they'd manage to steal so much cash. *Maybe they had bitten off more than they could chew?*

One recently retired Flying Squad detective told reporters: "It will very quickly become apparent to the gang that they have so much cash it will cause them problems. The case is high profile, making it extremely risky for them to spend any of the money."

For the moment, however, the gang seemed to have disappeared into thin air. The police knew their inquiries over the following 48 hours would be crucial. They mounted a massive operation with more than 100 officers who were immediately ordered to work fulltime on the case. Their initial priority was to try and locate the vehicles and properties used in connection to the raid. Detectives believed these would most likely hold the key to the robbers' identities.

Meanwhile, the Bank of England asked for a review of the security arrangements for the storage of banknotes. Although a bank spokesman insisted: "There is no cost at all to the Bank (of England) or the taxpayer resulting from the heist."

Police quickly issued two photo-fit images. One was a robber wearing a policeman's cap and sporting a "wiry and wispy" ginger beard. This was as he had appeared when he kidnapped manager Colin Dixon.

The other photo-fit image showed the same man: white, about six feet tall and with freckles, but this time without the beard and cap. Detectives believed the beard was either false or that he would have shaved it off immediately after the raid.

Police also announced there was a £2 million reward on offer, and appealed to people "around the edge" of the criminal fraternity to come forward to help identify the blaggers.

Securitas duty manager Paul Fullicks described to reporters how the robbers had beaten up both him and the 13 other nightshift workers. He said the members of staff were suffering "varying degrees of shock" after their "brutal, horrific and traumatic" experience. Securitas immediately brought in trained counsellors to help the workers.

Meanwhile, depot manager Colin Dixon's anger and resentment about the treatment inflicted on his wife Lynn and his child, who'd only turned nine the previous Friday, grew. Staff empathized with him at how an innocent woman and a child could be treated so brutally.

Initially, police arrested two women and five men, but they were quickly freed on bail. Then officers detained a further five people for questioning, including another woman, all whom were believed to be "prime suspects".

It emerged that one of the men questioned was Chris Bowles, 49, a European and British judo champion and registered coach who competed in the 1980 Moscow Olympics. Speaking to the Press Association at his home in Hildenborough, near Tonbridge, Mr Bowles said after his release: "I'm in a really difficult situation and I'm not prepared to comment at this stage, other than the fact that I am helping police with their inquiries. As time goes by more will be revealed."

Ten other locations searched by police included the home of one of Mr Bowles's martial arts colleagues, kickboxing expert Lea Rusha, 33, from the Kent village of Southborough. Detectives suspected Rusha was one of the actual robbers.

Meanwhile, detectives arrested another woman after she walked into the Portman Building Society in Bromley, Kent, and tried to deposit almost £10,000 in cash. Bands around the banknotes bore serial numbers indicating they had come from the Tonbridge depot. The woman was detained on suspicion of handling stolen goods.

Gradually, vehicles linked to the robbery were located and forensic scientists began an inch-by-inch examination of them for clues and evidence. A red van with Parcelforce markings – found in a pub car park near the Tonbridge depot – was believed to have been used to transport Mrs Dixon and her child after they were abducted from their home in Herne Bay.

Colin Dixon's Nissan Almera – which he'd been driving home when the two bogus policemen stopped him – was discovered in the Cock Horse pub in the sleepy Kent village of Detling. The landlord said he'd not reported it initially because he assumed that one of his customers had left it there overnight.

Kent Police then "stumbled" on £1.4 million in cash from the robbery in a white Transit van in the car park of Ashford International Hotel. The van also contained a machine gun and a black balaclava with one of the suspect's DNA on it.

It was already clear that detectives were getting inside help, but they continued to keep their investigation very close to their chest. There was no way that all that cash and armoury would have been left in an abandoned vehicle. They must have had a tip-off in order to locate it. Detectives also discovered the burnt-out remains of the Volvo saloon – used as the "police car" – in Burberry Lane in the Kent village of Leeds, near Maidstone.

Within two days of the robbery, detectives pinpointed Elderden Farm as the location where the Dixons had most probably been taken in the hours before the robbery. Forensic experts, specialist search units and divers were soon swarming all over the isolated farm as the hunt for the gang behind the UK's biggest cash robbery gathered pace.

A police car blocked the entrance to the 400-metre private drive that led to the farm's main property, and officers marked off the entrance and perimeter with police tape. Dozens of uniformed officers, some with dogs, and forensic experts began a painstaking search of the main house and outbuildings for any clues, however small. Other officers conducted fingertip searches of the surrounding fields.

Police also brought in divers with ropes and equipment to examine a well near the house. Two 4x4 vehicles – a dark green Land Rover Discovery and a dark blue Range Rover

– plus a Vauxhall Vectra saloon were taken away from the farm for forensic examination.

Then police found a green Peugeot abandoned in a barn on the property. It contained £30,000 cash in Securitas wrappers in the boot. They also found a black binliner concealed beneath some logs at the base of a dead tree in an orchard. It contained £105,600.

Andrew Hutchinson, landlord of the Lord Raglan pub in Staplehurst, told reporters the owner of the farm was a familiar face in the village tavern, but that he had not seen him since the previous week. Initially, Kent Police would not confirm if the farm's owner was being questioned. Detectives then recovered a 7.7-ton white Renault Midlum lorry, which the robbers had used to load with cash during the early morning raid. The lorry had been captured on CCTV as it left the depot following the robbery.

The owner of Elderden Farm was eventually cleared of any involvement in the Securitas robbery. During the robbers' later trial, it was alleged that the Dixons were held at the property, but the owner has always denied this claim.

The investigation continued at a pace. Police had rapidly established a number of crucial facts. A few weeks before the robbery, so-called "inside man" Hysenaj made a covert video of the inside of the Securitas depot using a video camera no bigger than a 50p piece fixed to his belt. Officers knew this because it had been discussed between two suspects who had accidentally recorded a conversation on one of their mobile phones, which had been found shortly after the robbery.

Detectives also uncovered that, a few days before the raid, one robbery suspect twice visited a specialist security shop called Eyetec, in Chesterfield, to buy covert miniature cameras and recording equipment, used in the reconnaissance of the depot. Another one of the robbers had carried out similar reconnaissance at the home of Securitas manager Colin Dixon in Herne Bay, Kent.

Detectives even found a video recording of the reconnaissance of the Dixons' home at one suspect's address in Southborough, Tunbridge Wells, Kent. The following day, another suspect was arrested in Whitstable, Kent after armed police shot out the tyres of a BMW he was driving.

The net was rapidly closing in on the robbers.

Detectives then located hairdresser and make-up artist Michelle Hogg, who'd completed the prosthetic disguises for the robbers. She would later claim she had no idea what the men were planning.

Two suspects were then arrested after police shot out the tyres of their black VW Beetle in Deptford, south-east London.

On 2 March 2006, suspected inside man Hysenaj was arrested in Crowborough, East Sussex. Shortly afterwards, police uncovered £9.7 million of the robbery cash at the ENR garage in Welling, Kent. Three days later, police discovered £8.6 million at a lock-up garage in Southborough, Kent, which had been rented by one of the suspect's cousins.

Detectives had expected a long, complex enquiry, but clue after clue about the robbery seemed to be landing on the police's lap. It was, as one officer later said, "As if someone out there wanted us to catch these fellas as quickly as possible."

Soon, investigators had charged all but four of the entire alleged robbery gang. The two chief suspects had fled the

UK soon after the raid. They were cage-fighters Lee Murray and his school friend Paul Allen from south London. Murray had used the ring name "Lightning" and was renowned for dressing in an orange boiler suit wearing a Hannibal Lecter-style mask.

Murray was renowned for loving the good life and had been a regular at parties attended by such luminaries as *Big Brother* star Jade Goody, footballer Jermaine Jenas, Callum Best and page-three model Lauren Pope. Murray drove a yellow Ferrari Modena 360 and thought nothing of blowing thousands of pounds on evenings in West End casinos.

But Murray's one mistake in the aftermath of the robbery came when he accidentally pressed the record button on the handset of his mobile phone during a conversation about the robbery with fellow blagger Lea Rusha. The phone was later recovered and used by prosecutors to convict Rusha and other suspects.

Murray and Paul Allen had fled the UK straight after the robbery. First they travelled to Amsterdam, before then driving south through Spain to Morocco. For a while the two friends lived the good life in the capital Rabat, staying in a villa in the expensive part of town, going out clubbing at night, taking cocaine and spending heavily in the Megamall – Rabat's flashy shopping centre. But, unwittingly, they were drawing attention to themselves. It was rare in Morocco for single men to be sharing a house and the locals assumed they must be gay.

They were also spending large sums of money in the local casino – a classic money-laundering tactic – where it was possible to buy £100,000 worth of chips and cash them in for different money a few hours later. Then they drew the attention of local police, following allegations they'd beaten up a Moroccan after an argument.

On 25 June 2006, in a joint operation with Moroccan police, Murray and Allen were arrested at their favourite shopping mall in Rabat's Souissi district. Police said in a statement that they'd been tracking the two robbery suspects for three months. But with no extradition treaty between the UK and Morocco, it was not possible for police to bring back the two alleged blaggers.

Moroccan police revealed that Murray had also been charged with possession of "hard drugs". An officer said this could complicate extradition proceedings because, in theory, Murray would have to serve time in Morocco first for any offences committed there.

By the end of 2006, the cost of Kent Police's investigation had already swelled to £6 million; they requested further aid from the Home Office.

In June 2007, the other Securitas robbers faced a trial at the Old Bailey. Sir John Nutting QC, prosecuting, opened the hearing by telling the court that the robbers were inspired by the lure of "luxury, ease and idleness" and were prepared to target the "innocent and vulnerable" to achieve it.

In the dock were: Lea Rusha, 35, a former roofer of Lambersart Close, Southborough, Tunbridge Wells, Kent; Stuart Royle, 48, a car salesman from Maidstone, who allegedly helped provide vehicles; Jetmir Bucpapa, 26, an Albanian from Tonbridge, was the said to be the link to the "inside man"; and Emir Hysenaj, 28, from Crowborough, East Sussex. Bucpapa also allegedly helped with reconnaissance. Roger Coutts, 30, a garage owner from Welling, was allegedly linked to the plot. They had denied charges of conspiracy to kidnap, conspiracy to rob and conspiracy to possess firearms.

Keith Borer, 53, a signwriter from Maidstone, charged only with handling stolen goods, was said to have helped with changing the identity of the van used in the kidnap of Mrs Dixon and her child. Michelle Hogg, 32, from Woolwich, admitted applying the prosthetic masks, but denied knowing what their intended use was.

The court heard about how the robbers' inside man, Emir Hysenaj, had recently started work at Securitas and he'd allegedly helped recce the depot and provided the home address of manager Colin Dixon, who himself later would tell the court the raid was "the worst night of my life".

The verdict came just under a month short of the two-year anniversary of the crime, on 21 February 2006.

Lea Rusha, Stuart Royle, Jetmir Bucpapa and Roger Coutts were given indeterminate sentences with a minimum of 15 years. Emir Hysenaj, the inside man who had previously worked at the depot, was jailed for 20 years. The jury later found signwriter Keith Borer not guilty of handling £6,100 of stolen Securitas money, something he had always denied.

Following the convictions, Kent Chief Crown Prosecutor Roger Coe-Salazar said: "This was a very serious crime which involved the kidnap of, and threats to, Mr and Mrs Dixon and their nine-year-old child by masked men armed with guns, as well as 14 employees being held at gunpoint.

This was not a victimless theft. The defendants put people's lives at risk just to serve their own greed and to enjoy a life of luxury and ease that the theft of the cash would have offered to them."

Coe-Salazar also warned against portraying the heist as an *Ocean's Eleven*-style caper, saying: "There is nothing romantic or victimless about a child being held at gunpoint by masked men. This was a dangerous, highly callous crime."

Back in Morocco, in 2009, suspected Securitas robber Paul Allen dropped his fight against extradition back to the UK and returned under armed guard to face his accusers. Murray – who was half Moroccan – insisted on continuing his fight from the North African country. British law enforcement authorities immediately began a campaign to try and persuade the Moroccan authorities to deal with Murray for his role in the Securitas robbery.

In June 2010, Allen, 31, was finally sentenced to 18 years for his part in the raid. Allen had admitted charges of conspiracy to rob, kidnap and possess firearms. He pleaded guilty on the basis that he was not one of the robbers who entered the depot, or one of the kidnappers, and that he did not handle any firearms.

Addressing Allen's role in the conspiracy, Mr Justice Penry-Davey said: "It is clear that as a long-term friend and associate of Murray and with knowledge of what was being planned, you played an active part in various aspects of the preparations for the raid."

A few weeks later, Lee Murray himself was jailed for ten years in Morocco for co-ordinating the Securitas robbery. His decision to stay in Morocco had paid off handsomely, because he faced shorter sentences than his co-robbers and with the right "connections" in Morocco he will probably be out on parole very soon.

AFTERMATH

Police are convinced that one Sean Lupton – whom they believe was a key player in the Tonbridge robbery – continues to hide in northern Cyprus with up to £32 million of the £53 million haul. A few years after the heist, the wife of the missing Securitas suspect told a tabloid newspaper that she believed Lupton had been lured to his own execution by an underworld hitman after a row over the stolen cash. Therese Lupton said she feared for her own life and produced a hand-written note threatening her 47-year-old husband. The anonymous letter, scrawled in black felt-tip pen, read: *Sean Lupton talks too much. Stole my money. Tonbridge robbery. People don't like it.*

So were his wife's claims just another bit of criminal trickery deliberately designed to put detectives off Lupton's "scent"?

Therese Lupton insisted that her husband was double-crossed and eventually killed by a dangerous gangland figure, known as Mr X, whom she now believed would come after her and their children. She claimed that in his final phone call, Lupton told her, "I won't be back for tea, but I'll see you later." She never saw her husband again.

But Therese did reveal that Lupton had watched the George Clooney film *Ocean's Eleven* about a casino robbery over and over again before the heist and that he was a "close associate" of the raid gang's van driver Stuart Royle. She also admitted that her husband was given £2.5 million to launder and confirmed Lupton had "connections" with the raid team.

Therese, a 47-year-old legal secretary, said "builder" Lupton vanished from their home in Whitstable, Kent, on 12 December 2006. Weeks earlier, he had been arrested on suspicion of plotting robbery and kidnap after 20 officers had stormed their house at dawn. But he was later released on police bail. That sparked rumours in the underworld that Lupton had "done a deal" with the police and may have resulted in a price being put on his head.

Therese said of their last day together. "Sean didn't act like a man about to go on the run. He woke the kids for school, but didn't kiss them or tell them he loved them. He doted on them and I'm sure he didn't think that was the last time he'd see them. He left without saying goodbye, but that was normal for him. At about 6pm, I called him to ask if he would be home for tea. He said no, but that he wouldn't be late. He told me he was going to see a very hard man, who I'll call Mr X. People are scared of him, but Sean had met him a few times.

"But when he didn't come home by 11.30pm, I knew something was wrong. I called him and his phone went straight to voicemail. At 6pm the next day I called the police."

Lupton's white van was found a month later at the Channel port town of Dover. Police believe Lupton fled to the Turkish part of Cyprus, which has no extradition treaty with the UK.

Therese says that when she eventually started asking questions among her husband's acquaintances, she was told a hitman had killed him. She also revealed that another criminal and her husband had each been given £2.5 million to launder and Therese told the tabloid she believed the robbers the police never caught are locked in a war about the money.

Therese Lupton even heard her husband talking on the phone to Stuart Royle following the heist. She said, "I heard them on the phone a lot and they would often meet at a local fish and chip shop. I was wary of Stuart, because I knew he had a previous conviction for fraud, but Sean told me not to worry."

However, Therese insisted her husband was not on the actual heist team because he was at home with her and their children – Jordan, 16, and Jasmine, 18 – on the night of the robbery. She said, "He picked Jordan up from a dancing class, and I was at a parents' evening. We watched TV, had a meal and went to bed at 11pm."

The following day, Sean Lupton joked when he saw news of the robbery on the TV and that the police's initial thoughts were that the gang came from his hometown. But Therese insisted her husband maintained his calm even when the other robbers were arrested. Therese said, "When Stuart Royle's name flashed up on the TV, Sean said, 'It must be a mistake, he can't have been involved.'"

Three weeks later, police arrested Lupton. "Sean was told he could get a T-shirt and on his way he passed Jasmine's room and saw her crying. But he didn't even flinch. Then he kissed me on the cheek, smiled and went with the police without showing any emotion."

Fourteen hours later Lupton arrived back home after being released on bail. Therese recalled: "He acted like nothing had happened. I bombarded him with questions, but he had an answer for everything. He said police were only interested in him because he knew some of the robbers."

Therese claimed that her marriage had been unhappy for years – and that if her husband was still alive in northern Cyprus, she would never join him as a fugitive.

"In a way I feel relief that he's not in my life now," she said. "I just wish that there was a body. I'm in limbo. I can't sell the house for eight years, when he can be declared dead, and I'm struggling to pay the mortgage. People think I'm a gangster's moll, but I actually hate him for what he's done to the children."

Less than a week after this interview was published, the riddle surrounding Sean Lupton deepened after witnesses said they'd seen him alive and well in northern Cyprus. Locals claimed the runaway villain had set up home in the tiny mountain village of Catalkoy.

Builder Turgay Adyin said, "I saw him drinking in the English bars – he's pretty stocky and looks like every other ex-pat, apart from his funny eye (Lupton has a lazy left eye). He was careful to make sure he was never out and about too much, but I know he was being looked after because there were always people with him."

A local taxi driver also came forward to tell how he was paid to help smuggle Lupton into northern Cyprus from the Greek-controlled south.

Police have always been convinced Sean Lupton was a key player in the Tonbridge blagging. Detectives are also seeking one other man, who they believe to be in the West Indies. In the eyes of many police officers and criminals, the saga of Britain's biggest-ever cash robbery remains unfinished business.

12. HIGH STAKES

"It seems from the nature of the robbery that these men are pretty well connected. They had a lot of cars, a lot of backup and support. It wasn't just an opportunistic heist – they are sophisticated."

One of the first detectives on the scene

Graff's jewellers, New Bond Street, Mayfair, London,
6 August 2009, 4.40pm

The two sharply dressed men, in virtually identical grey business suits, arrived in a taxi near Graff's jewellers in New Bond Street, Mayfair, Central London, just before the main rush-hour out of the city began. They were so cocky and confident, they even ensured the driver who dropped them off near the shop would remember them by paying the £9.20 fare with a £20 note, telling him to keep the change – the best tip he had ever received. The cabbie later said he thought they were Londoners.

The two men made no attempt to conceal their faces from the store's CCTV cameras either, because they believed their elaborate disguises would never give away their true identities. Even though one of the robbers was wearing leather gloves, store security, used to the eccentric behavior of many of Graff's super-wealthy clients, allowed him to stroll in. Once inside, they both pulled out handguns and forced staff to the floor of the store,

Shop assistant Petra Ehnar later recalled she was "petrified" when one of the robbers thrust a gun in her back and ordered her to empty rings, necklaces, watches and earrings from display cases. A total of 43 pieces of jewellery worth a total of £40 million was put into their bag. One diamond necklace alone was valued at £3.5 million and the haul included almost 1,500 individual diamonds.

CCTV footage from inside the store later showed manager Martin Leggatt spread-eagled on the floor with a gun pointed at his head. The other staff members were alongside him. Then, one of the robbers turned his gun back towards Petra and once again prodded her in the back, making it clear they were not finished with her yet. They then used Petra as a "shield" to guarantee their safe passage to a BMW getaway car waiting nearby.

The CCTV footage of the robbers leaving the store with Ms Ehnar at gunpoint, clearly shows the weapon pressed to her back as the robbers walk outside into the street and turn to the right where a blue BMW motor car waited to drive them away.

As one robber continued dragging the terrified woman at gunpoint into the crowded street, he drew further attention by firing at an approaching security guard, although the robber would later claim he used the gun purely to scare away the crowds. Once again, CCTV footage clearly shows the robber firing his gun as people in the crowded street started to gather around them. Petra Ehnar later testified that the robbers told her she would be killed if she did not carry out their orders.

Petra was only finally released on the street when the two raiders reached their blue BMW. Moments later, with a screech of tyres, it departed; the driver did not even wait for his fellow gang members to close their doors after they had jumped in.

Less than 30 seconds later, just around the corner in Dover Street, the BMW crashed into a black cab. As the men clambered out of the wrecked car, the taxi driver and customers from a nearby pub gave chase. That's when one of the robbers fired at least one more shot into the air to warn them off. Robert French, who had been having a "quiet pint" outside a nearby pub, had initially chased the men believing them to be hit-and-run drivers.

In their haste to transfer to a second vehicle – a silver Mercedes – a pay-as-you-go mobile phone was left wedged between the driver's seat and handbrake of the BMW. When the police later searched the boot of the car, they found a loaded sawn-off shotgun and four cartridges. Anonymous numbers stored on the mobile phone would eventually enable detectives to discover the identity of the robbers and track their movements.

Just after the robbers got into the second vehicle, the bag containing the 43 items of jewellery was handed to a motorcyclist on Stafford Street. However, the bike failed to start, forcing the rider to push it to the end of the street, where he finally abandoned it before disappearing on foot towards Green Park.

Next, the two robbers switched vehicles for a third time, on this occasion in Farm Street, Mayfair, and promptly disappeared into thin air. Witnesses later reported seeing the men flee in a black vehicle, possibly a Ford Galaxy or VW Sharan. There appeared to be at least two other men acting as getaway drivers for the three cars.

After the robbery, Detective Chief Inspector Pam Mace from Scotland Yard's Flying Squad told reporters: "This was a well-planned robbery with a number of vehicles used to help the robbers escape. These men are extremely dangerous and fired at least two shots in busy London streets as they made their getaway.

"Someone knows who these men are, they would undoubtedly have spoken about it beforehand or boasted about it afterwards. I would urge anyone who recognizes them, knows the whereabouts of the jewellery or has any other information to contact us."

The police described one suspect as white, about 30, with a slim build, dark hair with a well-combed side parting, light stubble on his face and between 5 feet 10 inches and 6 feet tall. He was wearing a grey suit, a white shirt and a tie. The second suspect was said to be black, also in his 30s, 6 feet tall, more well built than the first suspect, and with a very short Afro hairstyle. He was also wearing a grey suit, a white shirt and a tie.

Detectives had no doubt the raiders deliberately targeted the most expensive items in the store. One officer said: "They knew exactly what they were looking for and we suspect they already have a market for the jewels."

The suspects' details were immediately circulated to all ports and airports, but police admitted it was highly likely they had a carefully planned escape route and had probably already left the country.

All of the diamonds had been laser-inscribed with the Graff logo and a Gemological Institute of America identification number, but that would not prevent the gems from being easy to offload. Antonia Kimbell, from the Art Loss Register's recovery unit, explained: "Inevitably these items are highly portable, which makes it easier for them to be transported abroad. Often they are gone within hours. They would have been flown abroad immediately. When the jewellery leaves, it will pass through a number of hands very quickly to disassociate itself from the people who carried out the initial robbery."

Ms Kimbell continued: "The value of items when they are stolen is obviously always less than their market value. Typically, they might be traded for ten per cent of the market price, though there are several ways they can be sold on.

"The police have come across warehouses where items are melted down – the gold is melted and the gems are sold separately. Sometimes items are altered in a more minor way, just so they look different – especially if they are unique – before being traded.

"New jewellery is often laser marked, but that sometimes can be lasered off, depending on how sophisticated the robbers are. Sometimes the jewellery can even be sold on to people unchanged. If the robbers are very, very quick, they can be ahead of the checks made against such sales. For example, if they sell on the same day, so people don't realize the items are stolen. Or they can sell to an unscrupulous buyer or someone who is not careful to carry out the checks of legitimacy.

"However, the idea that jewellery might be stolen to order for someone's private collection is something we have never proved true – it's a Hollywood myth. Another use for the jewellery can be as a trading tool. These people tend to be associated closely with drugs or arms or other such things and this can be used as a way to trade for other items. Sometimes items can be hidden and remain in the country, but I think with the high-profile nature of this robbery that seems unlikely. Also, the people who carried out the raid are likely to have dispersed and gone abroad."

Meanwhile, police analyzed a series of anonymous numbers stored on the mobile the robbers had left in the BMW and quickly managed to establish that the gang had used several phones which they had bought in the lead-up to the heist. "The mobile phones were crucial for the police because they hoped that, eventually, the phones themselves would lead them directly to the robbers," said one retired Flying Squad officer.

In the hours following the heist, police released details of the cars used by the robbers. Scotland Yard also issued CCTV images of the two robbers dressed in suits and concealing handguns as they entered the store.

Then Flying Squad detectives got a tip-off that the two robbers had visited a Covent Garden make-up studio where they had duped professional makeup artists into "ageing" them, ostensibly for a pop video. The two men had their hair altered with wigs, their skin tones changed and their features distorted using latex prosthetics. A make-up artist took four hours to apply the disguise. Viewing the results in a mirror, one of the robbers – 25-year-old Aman Kassaye – commented: "My own mother wouldn't recognize me now," to which his accomplice is reported to have laughed and replied: "That's got to be a good thing, hasn't it?" The same make-up studio had also unwittingly helped disguise members of the gang that robbed a Securitas depot in 2006.

Later, however, the two men had pulled off the latex, complaining it did not look realistic enough, and decided instead to use greasepaint and powder.

The 29-year-old make-up artist who transformed the men was put under police protection within hours of the heist. DNA tests were also carried out on the masks the robbers had tried on in the studio but did not use.

Detectives also quickly found the broken-down high-powered motorbike intended to be used to spirit away the bag holding the stolen gems until it failed to start. And within 24 hours of the raid, detectives also raided at least three properties in London and the South-East.

But it was the mobile phone left in the BMW that was the clincher. It led police directly to Ethiopian-born robbery mastermind Aman Kassaye, a drug-dealing media studies student who had dropped out of St Mary's University College, Twickenham.

Within six weeks, as many as ten male suspects – including Kassaye – had been arrested in connection with the robbery. Charges brought against the individuals included conspiracy with others to commit robbery, attempted murder, holding someone hostage, possessing firearms and using a handgun to resist arrest.

At the robbers' eventual trial, Woolwich Crown Court heard how gang leader Kassaye and his associate Craig Calderwood were the robbers who had raided Graff's and terrified both staff and members of the public in this so-called "high-stakes" raid.

The jury of eight women and four men were shown a passing pedestrian's mobile phone footage of raised voices and shouting outside the jewellers; a moment later, a shot rings out in the street outside the store as passers-by began to realize what was happening and ran for cover.

Besides Calderwood and Kassaye, Soloman Beyene, 25, Clinton Mogg, 42, Courtney Lawrence, 31, Gregory Jones, 30, Thomas Thomas, 45, David Joseph, 23, and Benjamin McFarlane, 22, all denied conspiracy to rob. Calderwood and Kassaye each denied possessing a handgun and a sawn-off shotgun. Kassaye also denied kidnapping the store assistant.

After viewing the footage taken outside the store, prosecuting counsel Philip Bennetts told the jury: "It introduces you, does it not, to something of the atmosphere of that day and what those in the store would feel when guns were shown and they were threatened when they were forced, as they were, to hand over the jewellery… The end result is that those involved succeeded in their goal.

"The terrified employees handed over the jewels, people who attempted to impede the escape were shot at, and the bag containing the jewels was handed to a waiting motorcyclist who would have made his escape if his machine had not broken down."

Mr Bennetts insisted the victims were "the real centre of this case, not the value of jewels that were taken". They were "the victims of a terrifying robbery at gunpoint", he added.

Gang leader Kassaye watched the footage from the secure dock at the back of the packed courtroom, along with the other eight defendants. But co-robber Calderwood stared at his feet while the images of their heist were screened.

The jury heard the robbery had originally been supposed to take place two days before the actual crime was committed. This was proved when images of both men wearing disguises were caught on CCTV on 4 August. The men could clearly be seen looking into the Graff's window but, it seemed, their plans were abandoned when a routine police patrol car drove past them twice over a short period of time.

Kassaye, however, denied he was the black robber caught on CCTV during the attempted robbery and actual heist two days later. He did admit he bore a resemblance to the man, but insisted the real robber was a man called "Omar" and Kassaye claimed he'd been framed. Calderwood, on the other hand, admitted he was the white man caught on the CCTV, but insisted he'd been forced to take part.

The court also heard that gang member Beyene was a university graduate and convicted drug dealer released from prison just a month before the robbery. He purchased the phones used for the raid and hired a Ford Transit van used to block police pursuing the BMW as it made its getaway.

Defence counsel Courtenay Griffiths QC then dropped a legal bombshell by suggesting that Graff store manager Martin Leggatt was the gang's "inside man". CCTV footage had shown Leggatt spread-eagled on the shop floor during the robbery. But when Griffiths faced Leggatt in the witness box, he told him: "I don't want there to be any illusions between us, I am going to suggest that this robbery in August last year was an inside job and that you were involved in it."

Mr Leggatt dismissed the claim as "a conspiracy theory". He said: "I would be absolutely fascinated to hear your evidence for that."

Griffiths – one of London's best-known defence barristers – told Woolwich Crown Court that Graff Diamonds, owned by Laurence Graff – known as the "King of Bling" and the "Lord of the Rings" – had been subjected to a series of previous robberies at his stores all over the world, during which jewellery worth tens of millions of pounds had been stolen.

Mr Griffiths listed raids in 1980, 1993, 2003, 2004, 2005, 2007 and 2009, including a $38 million (£24.5 million) raid at a Graff's store in Toyko, a $13.5 million heist in its Dubai store and £20 million stolen from the company's Sloane Street location in London's Knightsbridge.

Griffiths told the court that two men wearing disguises "nearly always" conducted these raids and – on each occasion – substantial amounts of jewellery were stolen. Griffiths alleged in court that Graff stores were "specialists in being robbed". Griffiths continued: "There just appears to be recurring bad luck for Mr Graff. He just seems to be getting robbed all the time of millions of pounds worth of jewellery."

"Thank you for your sympathy," replied Leggatt, who'd worked for Graff for 17 years.

Griffiths then told the court that immediately after the New Bond Street robbery, one shop assistant told police the gems stolen were worth £20 million, but later reports doubled that initial estimate.

"Do you understand where I'm coming from?" Griffiths asked Mr Leggatt.

"I've got a horrible feeling I do, yes," replied Mr Leggatt, who said he did not know the exact value of the jewellery taken.

Griffiths then asked Leggatt why security guards at the store had not pressed the alarm button to alert the security firm until 4.43pm, at the end of the two-and-a-half minute raid, by which time the robbers had escaped. Griffiths also wanted to know why a smoke alarm that would have filled the shop with dry ice had not been activated.

Leggatt told the court he could only surmise it was to avoid "a massacre" inside the store, which could easily have occurred with two armed men shooting randomly in a room so thick with dry ice and smoke that "no one could see anything".

Barrister Griffiths then asked Leggatt: "Was it for strategic operational reasons like, 'Let's not call the police until after this set-up robbery has taken place?'"

Leggatt replied: "I really relish the chance to listen to your conspiracy theories."

Griffiths also questioned Leggatt about his boss's financial affairs. Griffiths asked if he was aware that, because of the credit crunch, "Mr Graff was sitting on a load of unsold diamonds". Griffiths also alleged Graff had "bought half-a-million shares" for £28.5 million in a company called Gem Diamonds on 13 November 2008, but that within four days of that purchase "the share price dropped by 35 per cent, so he lost upwards of £10 million".

Griffiths also alleged that both owner Graff and his wife "sold their shares in Graff one month after the robbery". Leggatt replied by saying he was a shop manager and that he had no knowledge of Graff's share portfolio.

Questioned later by Ian Bourne QC, representing robbery suspect Calderwood, over the same inside-job allegations, Leggatt replied: "It seems rather one-sided for you to make these allegations, which I find incredibly offensive, incredibly unfounded and totally without justification. It's totally unfair your learned friends are able to say this without any back-up whatsoever."

The jury, of eight women and three men, convicted Kassaye – the gang's ringleader – of conspiracy to rob, kidnapping and possessing a gun.

Beyenne was convicted of conspiracy to rob by a majority verdict, as was Clinton "Jamal" Mogg, who provided the flat used by Kassaye and Calderwood to have themselves aged by a professional make-up artist on 4 August, the date of the dry run or failed attempt, which was caught on CCTV cameras outside the New Bond Street store.

Thomas Thomas, of East Finchley, who hired a 7.5-ton truck used to block traffic during the getaway, was convicted by a 10–1 majority of conspiracy to rob.

But the jury was unable to reach a verdict on alleged robber Craig Calderwood, who admitted taking part in the raid, but claimed he was forced into it by threats to kill him and his mother from two underworld figures known as "Kev" and "The Big Boss". At Calderwood's later re-trial, he was found guilty for his part in the robbery

Courtney Lawrence, of Holland Park, west London, and David Joseph, of Camberwell, south London, were cleared of conspiracy to rob after denying involvement. Two other men – Gregory Jones, of Maida Vale, west London, and Benjamin McFarlane, of Marylebone, north-west London – were also cleared of the same charge.

On 7 August 2010, robber Kassaye was sentenced to 23 years in prison. Beyene and Thomas Thomas were each jailed for 16 years after being convicted of conspiracy to rob. At the later re-trial, Calderwood was sentenced to 21 years.

AFTERMATH

Experts remain convinced the haul of gems from the New Bond Street store were probably broken up so the stones could be laundered back into the diamond market after being re-cut.

"The most obvious identification is the weight and the physical dimensions of the stones," jeweller Harry Levy, the vice-president of the London Diamond Bourse, said. "All these can be altered by re-cutting. As far as most stones go, once you change the weight and change the dimensions it would be very, very difficult for them to be re-identified."

Levy said those behind the robbery would have aimed to change the stones and sell them, albeit for less than their original value. "The likelihood is they would not put them out on the well-known western markets," he said. "But they could go out in China, Hong Kong, India, Russia or the Middle East, where there are strong markets and plenty of money. And the people who buy them probably won't go to the length of trying to identify them. It's not in their interest."

One diamond, stolen during another, earlier, June 2007 robbery at the same New Bond Street store, eventually turned up in a Hong Kong pawnshop. It was then shipped to New York for closer examination where it was kept under lock and key, prompting Graff to sue for its return.

The more than 16-carat yellow diamond had been stolen when two smartly dressed men stepped out of a Bentley Continental Flying Spur limousine, pretending to be shoppers and chatted up store staff before producing handguns and stealing diamond-and-gem-studded rings, necklaces, pendants and earrings.

The diamond found in Hong Kong was the first and only piece recovered from that earlier robbery. The Hong Kong pawnshop submitted the diamond for certification to the Gemological Institute of America, according to a lawsuit later filed by Graff's at the New York Supreme Court in Manhattan. The Institute had certified the diamond before the robbery and determined that it was the same one, albeit re-cut.

Graff's insisted it "is and was the true owner of the diamond and was entitled to immediate possession of the diamond", but the pawnshop would not let the Institute return it. The court papers did not give a value. The Institute refused to discuss the matter because of the dispute, but it regularly works with police when stones were reported lost or stolen.

It was reported at the time that Graff Diamonds lost more

than $10 million (£6.6 million) as a result of the New Bond Street robbery. For insurance purposes, the actual value of the pieces was put at $39 million (£26 million). However, according to Nicholas Paine, the company secretary, the syndicate that insured Graff was only liable for $28.9 million.

While those convicted executed the raid, it was believed the underworld bosses who planned and financed the heist remain at large to this day.

POSTSCRIPT

In south London, they still reckon that when the Great Train Robbery Gang were banged up for those long sentences, the mugging rate doubled overnight, because whatever those notorious robbers might have been up to, their presence discouraged the small-timers. The truth is that London's old-style blaggers of the 1950s and '60s were a very different bunch from today's organized criminals. In those days, the big names were outlaws, of course, but they were seen as a stabilizing influence within their communities. Their power inspired respect, not just among rival villains, but also among petty crooks, who might otherwise have been tempted to prey on people on the "manor". Across the river in east London, the Kray twins also ruled with a similar styled iron hand. "No one would dare mug an old lady on Ronnie and Reggie's manor," one old timer told me a few years back.

Back then the *really heavy gangsters* were high profile and far less subterranean than the sinister, anonymous characters around today. The Krays went to first nights, cultivated sporting and West End stars. In their heyday in the early 1960s they were often seen with some of the most glamorous people in London and regularly had their picture in London's newspapers. Today's Godfathers prefer to stay in the shadows, while secretly financing blaggings and drug deals galore. Few really know them and, unlike their more colourful predecessors, no one wants to know them.

Today, Britain remains in the grip of organized crime. Law-abiding citizens think of robbers and drug dealers as a bunch of seedy, unshaven youths hanging out on street corners flogging crack. The truth is that many of them actually live in detached mansions, drive £50,000 motors and send their children to public schools. Others are from places as far afield as Albania and Afghanistan – and few of them are here under their real names.

But there's no doubt that heists are helping fuel many of the killings on Britain's streets. A few years ago, a gunman with a grudge against another robbery gang let rip at dozens of innocent people lining up outside Chicago's nightclub, in Peckham, south-east London, in the early hours of the morning, injuring nine people, including a 16-year-old kid. The attack was blamed on Yardie gangsters and it didn't even get a mention on the TV news the following day.

The statistics speak for themselves: at least 200 murders a year in the UK can be linked to organized crime, which, in turn, is fuelled by robbery and drugs. And hundreds more are hurt in shootings like the one in Peckham. Then there are the robbers who disappear without trace after being chopped into little pieces by their enemies. Even the old-school Cockney blaggers say that the situation has "got completely out of fuckin' control" in the past ten years. Younger, often foreign, under-40 robbers are threatening the peace and stability that the older criminal faces will always claim they helped promote.

As one retired London detective recently told me: "We took the attitude that every time there was a hit that meant one less villain on the streets – and that can't be a bad thing. The robbers, in particular, kept to their own territory and didn't threaten the main population. But these new, deadlier foreign criminals have always got someone waiting in the wings and they don't respect territories or other human beings. It's going to take a hell of a police force to stop them ruling our streets."

The trouble is that crime thrives regardless of the financial state of a nation. There will always be young men out there happy enough to carry a gun to ensure they can pull off a robbery. It's as flash as playing for Chelsea or being a big-time fighter. It's showbiz. And as Legs Diamond said in the musical named after him: "I'm in showbiz, only a critic can kill me."

So where does all this robbery and violence leave us? There'll always be the Ganglands of Britain; the police know that and merely wonder how to prevent its tentacles spreading even further. These days the police are more reluctant to get in among the criminals like they did in those far-off days of legendary blags such as the Great Train Robbery. Today, the chances of planting an undercover cop in the most potent gangs of robbers are very slim. Budgets, politics and so-called ethics have all played a role in changing the rules of the game.

For at least the last 50 years the emphasis has been on trying to understand the habits of the robbers and that is what, to a certain extent, I've tried to do in this book. Are these characters really "born criminals" or did they develop those instincts from the circumstances upon which they were brought up as children? Many have attempted to prove that criminal characteristics are inherited. Others will argue, on almost Marxist terms, that "society has the criminals it deserves". In other words, society causes crime.

But then crime is undoubtedly a mental activity. Criminals such as legendary old timers like Mad Frankie Fraser and Freddie Foreman made a choice, which doesn't necessarily mean they could do anything to stop it. Those early days of abject hunger sparked within them a need to get out of control and led to anti-social behaviour, which manifested itself in many different forms from sexual to financial. But a robber's most significant incentive is the hunger for recognition, for admiration, a desire to be respected. All of us have this innate need, but it looms abnormally large within the underworld.

That hunger for recognition is a psychic need. In his book, *Anatomy of Human Destructiveness*, Erich Fromm calls it: "The need to make a dent." These characters want the world to know they exist. That demand for more life is all consuming and often at other people's expense. One member of the Great Train Robbery gang once told me that he could never match the buzz he felt as they were throwing those mailbags containing all that cash into their getaway lorry. This is that very mechanism of hunger at work. It is a fact of human psychology, which cannot either be condemned or approved.

It is a simple fact of life. The problem is that it can manifest itself in either a positive or negative fashion. In its positive form, it leads to entrepreneurs and captains of industry, but in others it ends in the ultimate risk-taking enterprise – crime, and in particular big-time heists.

In simple terms, the really serious blaggers – whatever their race, colour or creed – refuse to accept life as they find it. They don't just want to steal an apple from a tree; they want to burn the orchard down as well. Criminals are the archetypal scavengers, always on the lookout for an opportunity. They also suffer badly from long bouts of boredom and depression that can only be conquered by committing a crime.

Most career robbers often feel stifled and trapped, viewing stealing and sometimes even violence as the only means of escaping from the straightjacket. In many ways, their existence is a chain reaction, which can only end in their death or imprisonment.

Men and women like this don't need to stub their toe to react. They are constantly on tenterhooks, prepared to hit back at society because they don't feel they owe it anything. They never see themselves as being in the wrong and if they did say sorry, it would be an unnatural response in a moment of weakness, which they'd later regret.

For the serious robbers truly are the strangers among us, never one of us. Many labels have been hung on them over the years, but they don't tell half the story. Yes, they are often rebels and psychopaths: two shorthand symbols for a state of mind which is hate. Freud said that if a baby had power, it would destroy the world from the frustration of its infantile desires. In some ways, criminals represent that baby, who quite simply never grew up. That's why they feel so superior to everyone around them.

At the height of their criminal prowess, the rules of the game are being constantly challenged. Yet young criminals need rules to ensure their lives have some meaning just like everyone else. Their aggressive instincts are undoubtedly born out of sheer frustration with the world. It all seems so meaningless to them. There's that feeling of hopeless drifting. As their crimes start to bring them previously unimagined wealth, they also commit some offences like stealing cars purely for the thrill. But even in this environment there is a criminal structure constantly evolving. Codes and rank within a gang are obeyed to the letter. This is also a classic example of youths seeking a purposeful group identity.

So, the up-and-coming teams of robbers, like so many before and since, react partly against their own feelings of inadequacy. They are basically self-destructive, because their life has no real purpose despite often loving their wives and children and remaining married for their entire adult lives.

Throwing them into prison does little to stem the problem: big-time blaggers intrinsically lack the normal psychological vitamins. Their entire life is an act of hunger. To treat them properly requires a careful examination of their development and the details behind their crimes. Hopefully that's been achieved in this book. Punishment is wasted on most professional robbers. It is no better than caging an animal demented by hunger and expecting it simply to reform. The kind of hunger these characters often suffered from simply breeds a terrible hatred that feeds on itself.

One of the most ominous developments in the UK underworld

recently has been the apparent "joining forces" of once-sworn enemies. Bulgarian and Kosovan Albanian gangsters, for example, are rumoured to be working together with Turks to spearhead a surge in heists because they consider Britain to have so many rich pickings. Some have even linked up with specially trained Czech electronic experts in order to improve their technical capabilities when it comes to big-time blaggings.

Police even admit they are often powerless to act against many of the gangs' leaders, because they often remain back in their homelands orchestrating these jobs by phone and on the Internet. A classic example is one Turkish gangster who played professional football in Turkey and Canada before the enormous explosion in soccer wages. Following his retirement, this shadowy character set up a business exporting London "black cabs" to Turkey and also dabbled unsuccessfully in the property market. Then, Turkish gangsters in north London suggested he try drugs and robbery as a simple way of recouping his losses, so he set himself up in Istanbul and ran teams of robbers targeting Central London and Manchester.

The same man employed dozens more young Turks in north London to carry out his orders and to liaise with the robbery gangs. The Turkish gang boss then flew regularly between Turkey, Turkish-run northern Cyprus and London to make sure his teams of robbers were performing their "duties". This Turkish man is believed to have earned in excess of £6 million since 2007. However, one of his contacts brought the man to the attention of Customs and Excise investigators, who put him under surveillance and he was eventually brought to justice just before his most deadly team of robbers was about to strike in the City of London.

In another example of international gangster co-operation, London-based Turkish drug traffickers are said to be recruiting Bulgarian-organized crime gangs to protect their drugs shipments en route through Europe to the UK capital and then, when they arrive in UK cities, they pull off major armed robberies before fleeing back to their homeland.

Naturally, this virtually non-stop influx of foreign-based criminals into the UK has many disturbing knock-on effects. In London, the Metropolitan Police estimates that foreign gangs are carrying out at least one kidnap and/or robbery every day. These gangs also regularly use violence and torture to extract ransoms connected to drug deals.

The Flying Squad say that many of London's foreign gangs are a law unto themselves when it comes to robbery. And it's not always big-money crimes that are pulled off, either. In 2005, Lithuanian criminals snatched one of their fellow countrymen from a London pub, beat him senseless and then used his mobile phone to demand a £200 ransom from his family. When detectives eventually traced the victim, he was so badly beaten he had to spend weeks on a life-support machine before recovering.

The excessive use of firearms on the streets of big UK cities in recent years continues to provoke a deadly response from the police. In Edgware, north-west London, in April 2005, Azelle Rodney, 24, of west London, a passenger in the rear seat of a car, died when police opened fire on the vehicle. The car had been under surveillance by the Met as a result of intelligence, which suggested the driver and passengers were in possession of firearms and intended to carry out a robbery. Three loaded and fully operational guns were later recovered from the car. An investigation followed, but the Crown Prosecution Service said there was insufficient evidence to prosecute the police. The two other men in the car with Rodney later admitted firearms offences.

It's widely reckoned the Brink's-Mat villains brought more cash into this country than any other gang of criminals in history. And when they spent it, they often helped keep legit businesses afloat in the poorer areas of south-east London, as well on Spain's Costa del Sol.

And even the police themselves admit that they didn't really make life difficult enough for the Brink's-Mat team. Detectives only ever laid their hands on about 30 per cent of the stolen gold at most. The rest of it has gone up more than 100 fold in value since the 1983 heist.

But the Brink's-Mat heist is acknowledged to have been the turning point for an era of British crime. Robbery was overtaken by far more lucrative, less-risky enterprises such as drugs, arms dealing, racketeering and even people smuggling. And then, of course, there are the previously mentioned hoards of foreign criminals pouring into the UK. These cold-blooded characters are not interested in the professional standards shown by the McAvoys and Robinsons of this world.

Many of south-east London's oldest faces have slipped quietly out of the criminal limelight in recent years with no obvious British successors waiting in the wings. Many parts of south-east London have been gentrified and, in many cases, the children of those old-school robbers have ended up in straight jobs, often encouraged by their fathers – most of whom will happily admit that crime really doesn't pay. As legendary Krays' associate Freddie Foreman says: "We want our kids to have honest jobs and happy lives, not going in and out of prison and living in fear of a knock on the door. That's not the life I ever wanted for my kids and I've gone out of my way to make sure they avoided all my pitfalls."

Many villains from the Brink's-Mat era believe things have got completely out of control in recent years. One gang member said: "It's not like it used to be. A lot of these new foreign gangs are run by ruthless characters who wouldn't hesitate to kill their own mothers if they got in their way." Many of the younger, under-40 gangsters are threatening the peace and stability that used to be provided by many of those older faces.

One former detective, who spent five years working on the Brink's-Mat inquiry, is convinced that at least two gangs of younger robbers are now trying to find the missing Brink's-Mat gold. And they have started "breaking a few arms" in a bid to locate it. As one retired Flying Squad detective explained: "The old-boy blaggers of yesterday are slipping into the background now, but the kids know that gold is still somewhere out there and they've decided to do everything in their power to find it."

So what of the future? Will any of those old faces survive? And who is trying to muscle Britain's "profession" of robbery as we speak?

Millionaire criminals continue to try and corrupt and

compromise detectives, according to those who should know. It is claimed that police corruption has become even more of a problem today than it was during the Brink's-Mat era. It's estimated that there is a hard core of 250 "premier league" criminals at the top of the British underworld, many of whom are constantly tracked by the National Criminal Intelligence Service. This includes at least three members of the Brink's-Mat gang, still active after all these years.

Foreign crime-fighting agencies have warned Britain that the influx of gangsters into this country means that corruption is likely to escalate further into the new decade. The cold, harsh reality is that criminals will continue to thrive whatever governments try to do to eliminate them. Today, cyber crime has become the ultimate new version of robbery for the underworld. As one old face explained: "Going across the pavement was a risky enterprise in the old days. Now you can scam someone out of a fortune on the Internet without even leaving your front room. It's a different world out there."

Although the Hatton Garden heist of April 2015, dubbed the largest burglary in English legal history, would suggest otherwise, security systems are far more sophisticated today and few criminals would see the sense in such a high-risk operation. We're left with the aftermath of legendary robberies that continue to reverberate to this day.

As one detective so rightly commented: "A lot of the money and gold from those jobs is still out there and, until it's all recovered, there will be lot of people out there who believe that such audacious crimes owe them a living."

So it seems the globalization of the world's economic and information infrastructure has helped create a new, organized gangster elite in the UK. Many villains are covering their tracks with a vast array of legal businesses established as a front for their transnational underworld activities. Even the term "organized crime" is rapidly being replaced by "organized global crime". UK police believe that terrorists already turn to criminals to provide forged documents, smuggled weapons and clandestine travel assistance.

Fraud is big business in Britain because there are numerous people looking to make a quick and easy buck out of the misfortune of others. It is estimated that Britain is suffering about £3 billion a year in losses through fraud and other forms of economic crime and criminal gangs are even infiltrating the nation's banking industry.

And that means new kinds of robbers are emerging. One small gang based in London today specializes in stealing multi-million-pound pieces of art.

"It's much easier than walking into a bank and a painting is easy to transport. No wonder these sort of blaggings are on the increase," explained one old-time London robber. Most major museums have tight security, but there are still many places holding high-value works that have disproportionately poor security measures, making them susceptible to theft. But the ownership of high profile art is easy to track, so potential buyers are very hard to find. In the summer of 2003, a London gang stole a Leonardo da Vinci painting thought to be worth about £30 million from a Scottish castle. Nothing has been heard of the picture since, but art experts believe the gang who stole it was from London and may be sitting on it until a suitable buyer is found.

But the most ominous modern development of the robbery phenomenon is the Internet. With wi-fi hotspots popping up all over the UK, the gangsters' ability to tap into computers has improved drastically. People using wireless, high-speed Internet connections are being warned about fake hotspots or access points. Once a user has logged onto such a hotspot, sensitive data can be intercepted and money stolen. "It's the perfect robbery. No one gets hurt and the victim doesn't even realize he or she has been robbed until it's too late," explained one old-time London blagger, sounding envious.

Meanwhile, many of the old-time blaggers would rather take the secrets of their biggest crimes with them to their graves. Some cash in on their crimes through films and books about their lives, but many of the really powerful ones don't usually give much away. It's all part of a deeply rooted criminal philosophy developed while many of them were youths on the streets of Britain's big cities. "Never tell anyone a thing. Never give an inch."

Whatever the full extent of their power and influence over London life, these veteran blaggers reveled in their image as the romantic *crims*. They wanted to prove that crime really does pay, even though, as previously mentioned, most don't believe it does.

In many ways, the serious robbers of today work more like a business syndicate. Yet it mustn't be forgotten that most of them are perfectly willing to squeeze the trigger if required.

The old timers used to love pitting their wits against Scotland Yard and its worldwide reputation for skill and dogged determination. They nearly always considered they had one big advantage over the long arm of the law; the police had to work within certain rules and regulations. They, on the other hand, could do whatever they wanted.

For these legendary characters, robbery with violence was their raison d'être. They'd grown up in gangs where a fight was the natural means to settle a dispute and they could never truly appreciate the middle class's abhorrence of violence. Many have a selfish drive to escape from the slums of their childhood.

But there is an intriguing core of loyalty from many of their associates. Even virtual strangers come to them with information, often not even wanting any money or even a drink, but because they enjoyed helping their battle against the police. As E.J. Hobsbawm wrote in his book, *Bandits*: *"The crucial fact about the bandit's social situation is its ambiguity. He is an outsider and a rebel, a poor man who refuses to accept the normal rules of poverty and establishes his freedom by means of the only resources within the reach of the poor: strength, bravery, cunning and determination. This draws him close to the poor; he is one of them. It sets him in opposition to the hierarchy of power, wealth and influence: he is not one of them."*

As outlined in this book, since the Great Train Robbery in 1963, many UK police officers have been thrown out of the force for corruption, having fabricated evidence and dropped charges in exchange for cash. A lot of this overt corruption convinced many of Britain's criminals back then that their crimes weren't so bad. Yet throughout their life, these old timers showed total repugnance for the rules and formalities of the modern state – driving licences, permits, paying taxes, passports, even National Insurance Stamps.

Even the new crop of Britain's robbers from all over the world see themselves as the shock troops of the militant poor. That's why they often fall out with their own families, who, quite simply, do not understand where their children are coming from. Young and old criminals see obedience to the law and collaboration with the police as a betrayal of their own people, which would mean losing all self-respect.

Their obsession with money is usually fuelled by a desire for the better things in life: freedom, comfort, cleanliness, light, privacy and respect. But the good life they so desperately crave is never going to be paved with gold.

Violence is explained away as being "part of the game" or it's "what has to be done". Yet the evil that so many thought is endemic in many of the robbers featured in this book can be found in any of us and has little to do with the law of the land. There has always been a tendency to look back at a "golden era" of crime, as if there was once a magical time when no one got hurt, when crooks only attacked other crooks and when a strict code of honour ruled.

But times have changed and the re-explosion of robbery today in Britain provides an ominous insight about our future safety...

GLOSSARY

backhander – bribe
bang to rights – caught red-handed
bent – crooked
bang up – to imprison
bird – prison sentence
blag wages – snatch, robbery etc
blaggers – robbers
brass – prostitute
case – check out
chiv – a taped-up razor for cutting not stabbing
cop – receive a sentence
cozzer – policeman
DCI – Detective Chief Inspector
DCS – Detective Chief Superintendent
DI – Detective Inspector
dippers – pickpockets
drum – a flat or house
faces – renowned criminals
factory – police station
fence – criminal who sells stolen goods
finger – accuse
fitted up – framed
flophouse – hideout after robbery
folding money – banknotes
frummers – Orthodox Jews
grass – informer
guv'nor – senior policeman/gang boss
have one's collar felt – to be arrested
manor – territory of a villain or policeman
minder – bodyguard/troubleshooter

monkey – £500
Mr Wood – policeman's truncheon
old lag – long-term prisoner
pavement artist – robber
ponce – pimp
pony – £25
porridge – prison
run-in – secret location for unloading and storing stolen goods
scam – deception
screaming – informing to the police
screw – prison officer
screwsman – burglar or safe-breaker
shooter – gun
slag – smalltime crook
snout – informer / tobacco
spiv – a man who earns his money doing an honest day's work for a bookie
stretch – prison sentence
swallow – accept a situation without protest
Sweeney Todd – the Flying Squad
tealeaf – thief
team – regular gang of criminals
tearaway – small-time but generally violent and reckless criminal
tomfoolery – jewellery
tooled up – to be equipped with weapons for a crime
turned over – premises raided by police
verbals – report of "off-the-record" remarks made by villain to police
villain – crook of some standing

THE FINAL WORD – WATCH YER BACK

As you will have read, it's not the robberies themselves that so often lead to the arrest of the bad guys. It's how they turn their gold, jewellery and cash into actual *spending power*.

One of the world's most notorious blaggers once told me that after a lifetime of carrying out robberies, he's finally worked it out.

"First of all you get rid of any new, traceable notes. Chuck 'em away, but be realistic. And remember that whatever I say, the chances of success are extremely slim.

"Then bury the loot. Seriously. Put it somewhere you won't be going back to for months if not years. Don't go to a lock-up or a security vault. Find somewhere isolated and make sure you keep a careful record of where it is or else you'll be in trouble!

"Then, for as long as possible, forget about it completely. Hire yourself a decent financial advisor who knows both how to bend the rules and keep his mouth shut. Pay him well. Don't be tight about it, because otherwise he'll probably eventually grass you up.

"Then spend a tiny amount of the cash as a test, but keep it to small amounts of used notes only, in places such as dodgy casinos where nobody looks too closely at the cash. Don't be flash. Getting pissed up and pulling brasses is madness. They all know other villains and sometimes even the cozzers. Gradually get out bigger amounts and change them at dodgy looking *bureau de change* kiosks. Change the sterling into euros and then take those euros into Europe, through the

267

Tunnel or on the *Eurostar* train. But most important of all, stay calm and watch your mates carefully. Remember there will be a reward out there for anyone who grasses you up.

"Then find a bank somewhere in the world (Liechtenstein is good, I believe) where the law protects the identity of account holders, even from the coppers. But make sure you wait as long as you can before you do this. And if you are going to travel with large amounts of cash on you, go somewhere customs officials can be bribed to certificate your cash as clean.

"Then start a company. The Balkans is a good place to do that or maybe Dubai. Then begin very gradually transferring the money slowly into a tax haven, such as the Cayman Islands, where secrecy is assured. Set up a blind trust and nobody will know it's for you and then start transferring back the cash to the UK through more shell companies.

"Then set up an apparently legitimate business here. And hope nobody asks why it never goes bust. Or you could spend it on property, diamonds or whatever. Then, finally, sell up, and, hey presto, all your money is now clean.

"Oh and don't forget to close down all those dodgy accounts and make sure you haven't left a paper trail. See? It's a piece of cake (NOT).

"But remember, money poisons people's minds, so watch yer back, because a lot of vermin will come out from behind the woodwork and try to 'convince you' that part of your money belongs to them."

INDEX

A
Adams Family (A Team) 133, 176
Adams, Robert (Bob "The Builder")
    166–78
Adams, Terry 133–4
Alcock, James 95
Allen, Paul 223-24, 226
Anatomy of Human Destructiveness 252
Arif, Dogan 133
Art Loss Register 237
art theft 260

B
Baker Street (Walkie-Talkies Tell No Lies)
    55–68
Baldini, Enzo 147
Bandits 262
Bank Job, The 68
Banstead, Surrey (Taking the Mickey)
    69–86
Barclay, Gary 214
Benefield, Sammy (Chainsaw Gang
    member) 69–86
Bennetts, Philip 240–41
Bentley, Peter 104–7
Bermuda Triangle, Kent 129
Bestson, Raymond (Black Ray) 161–83
Bevins, Reginald 41
Beyene, Soloman 240, 241
Bhadresa, Manish 190, 192
Big One see Ledburn, Buckinghamshire
Biggs, Ronald Arthur (Ronnie) 31–53, 182
Bindon, John 66
Black, Tony 103–34
Blackwall Tunnel robbery, 1977 84–5
Borer, Ken 225
Bourne, Ian QC 244
Bowles, Chris 219
Bridego Railway Bridge 33
Brightwell, Tony 115–6
Brink's-Mat heist 100, 103–34, 257, 259
    see also The Big one
Brink's-Mat missing gold 119–34, 257, 258
Bristow, Jon 130
Bucpapa, Jetmir 225
Bully, The (Mickey McAvoy) 106, 107, 117
bungs 19
Butler, Tommy 19–20, 40, 42, 44–48, 51-2

C
Caccavale, George 121–2

Calderwood, Craig 233–47, 240
Calvey, Mickey 82
Calvi, Roberto 144
Cameron, Stephen 123
carjacking 182–3
Carter, Jack (Mr Big) 162, 180–2
Cartwright, Operation 194
Cater, Frank 41, 111, 116–7
Chainsaw Gang 69–86
Chapman, Ray 130
Ciarrocchi, Aldo 163
City of London (Snow over Shoreditch)
    87–101
Clarke, Ron 104, 106, 107
Cockram, William (Bill) 163–83
Coe-Salazar, Roger 225–6
Coombe, Judge Michael 178
Cordrey, Roger John 31–53, 46
Costa del Crime 100, 127, 133
Counsell, Greg 91–5
Coutts, Roger 225
Crime of the Century 103–34
Crime of the Decade 112
cyber crime 259, 261
Cyprus, Northern 133, 230–1

D
Daly, John 46
Davies, Edmund 49–50
De Beers Millenium Collection 161–83
De Beers mining company 163, 171–73
diamonds 139, 161–183
Dillinger, John 9, 11
Dixon, Colin 209–226
Dixon, Lynn 211–6, 218, 219
Dome Heist 161–83
Dovegate Prison 159
DPP (Director of Public Prosecutions) 21,
    114, 207
Drury, Kenneth 20–1

E
Eastcastle Street mail-van robbery, 1952 42
Edwards, Buster 33–53
Ehnar, Petra 234–35
Elderden Farm 213, 220, 221
Escobar, Pablo 125
Everett, Ronnie 87–101

F
Field, Brian Arthur 31–53

Field, Leonard Dennis   31–53
Finsbury bullion theft, 1960 42
Flying Squad, the 17–23, 170, 187, 236, 256
Foreman, Freddie 25, 27, 87–101, 160, 252, 258
Forman, Bill 81–84
Francis, George (Georgie Boy) 103–34, 132
Fraser, Mad Frankie 252
fraud 260
French, Robert 235
Fromm, Erich 252
Fronte della Giuventu 142
Fullicks, Paul 218

G
gangs (foreign) 23, 255–59
gangs (robbery) 13, 14, 254
Gavin, Anthony 67
Gentleman Thief, The, see Viccei Valerio
Gibson, Allan 120
Gladstone, Paul 217 see also The Big one
God's Banker see Calvi, Roberto 144
gold, Brink's-Mat missing 119–34, 257, 258
golden age of armed robbery 9
Goody, Douglas Gordon (Gordon) 31–53
Graff Heist, London 9, 11, 233-247*
Graff, Lawrence 242–44
Graff's Diamonds 234–47
Graff's Jewellers Mayfair (High Stakes) 233–47
Great Train Robbery, The 27, 31–53, 249
Green, Dr Andrew 159
Green, Mickey (The Pimpernel) 124–7
Greenwich, London (Operation Magician) 161–83
Grey Fox, the see Wickstead, Albert
Griffiths, Courtenay QC 241–44

H
Hale, Don 159
Hambrook, Walter 17
Hamill, James 123
Harrods 137
Heathrow Airport (Weak Spot) 185–95
heavy mob, the 17
Heslop, Martin 172–3
high jackings
High Stakes see Graff's Jewellers Mayfair
Hill, Billy 19, 25–7, 44, 53
HM Revenue and Customs 13, 255
Hobsbawm, E.J. 262
Hogg, Michelle 222
Holliday, Richard 104–8
Houslow, West London (Men on a Mission) 103–34

Huckerby, Graham 151–60
Humphreys, Jimmy 20–1
Hussey, James (Jimmy) 31–53
Hutchinson, Andrew 221
Hysenaj, Ermir 216, 221, 222, 225

I
informants 17–8, 21
  see also supergrasses
Innocent 159
IRA 197–208
Italian Stalion, The, see Viccei Valerio

J
James, David 169
James, Roy John (The Weasel 31–53
Jane's Defence Weekly 189
Jones, Gregory 240, 245
Joseph, David 240, 245

K
Kassaye, Aman 233–47, 240
Khan, Bernie (Chainsaw Gang member) 69–86
Kincaid, Sam 204
King of Bling see Graff, Lawrence
Kirsch, Elisabeth 176
KLM Airline Offices, Holborn 25–7
Knight, Chopper (Chainsaw Gang member) 69–86
Knight, John 87–101
Knight, Ronnie 87–101
Knightly, Tony (Chainsaw Gang member) 69–86
Knightsbridge Safe Deposit Centre 137–43, 149
Krays, The 19, 53, 88, 114, 249, 258

L
Lamont, Andrew 172
Latif, Parves 137, 143
Lawrence, Courtney 240, 245
Lawrence, Stephen 131–2
Lawson, Mickey 118
Le Sac shop, Baker Street robbery 64, 67
Leach, Dick 141, 144, 150
Leatherslade Farm 35, 39, 43, 45
Ledburn, Buckinghamshire 1963 (The Big One) 31–53
Leggatt, Martin 234, 241–44,
Limehouse Police Station 23
lip-reading 191–2
Lloyd, John 103–34
London Airport payroll snatch, 1959 42
London Diamond Bourse 245

INDEX

Lord of the Rings see Graff, Lawrence
Lupton, Sean 227–231
Lupton, Therese 227–30

M
M25 road rage death, 122, 123, 128
  see also Noye, Kenneth
MacArthur, Gerald 41
Mace, Pam 236
Malatesta, Antonio 146–8
Mason, Eric 31
Mason, John 100
McAvoy, Mickey (Mad Mickey) 103–34,
  257
McCann, Bob 121, 132
McFarlane, Benjamin 240, 245
McGuinness, Martin 206
McMullan, Karen 198, 204
McMullan, Kevin 198–9, 201
McShane, Gordon 14
media coverage 41–2, 44, 51, 64, 143, 189,
  205
Men on a Mission see Houslow, West
  London
Meredith, Kevin 168, 176, 178
Michael X 66, 67
Midland Bank Clearing Centre, Salford
  (Pointing the Finger) 151–60
Millennium Dome 161–83
Millennium Star diamond 161, 163, 166,
  172
Miller, Bill 118
Millman, Terry 164, 172, 175, 176
Mills, Jack 32–3, 48
Miscarriage of Justice Organization
  (MOJO) 159
Mobile Patrol Experiment 18
Mogg, Clinton (Jamal) 240, 244
money-laundering 13, 98, 133–34, 224
Moody, Jimmy 69–86, 89
Mother of all Robberies see KLM Airline
  Offices
Mr Big see Jack Carter 162, 180–2
Mr X 227, 228
Murphy, Niall 207
Murray, Lee 223–24, 226–7

N
Nardi, Gianni 142
National Crime Intelligence Service
  (NCIS) 13, 259
New Millennium Experience Company
  171–2
newspaper coverage 41–2, 44, 51, 64, 143,
  189, 205

Norris, Clifford 131–2
Norris, John 132
Northern Bank, Belfast (Who Played the
  Tune) 197–208
Noye, Kenneth 118, 119, 121–4, 127–9, 131,
  177
Nutting, Sir John QC 224

O
Ocean's Eleven 228
Ohio, Operation 81
Old Bailey 21, 47, 67, 172, 224
Operation Cartwright 194
Operation Magician see Greenwich,
  London
Operation Ohio 81
Operation Volga 156, 160
Orde, Hugh 205–6
Order 44 51
organized crime 10, 41, 256, 260
organized crime in Britain 53, 120, 146,
  249–51

P
Padda, Harbhajan 190
Palmer, John (Goldfinger) 131
Parkhurst Jail 143
Parmar, Anil 190, 191
Perkins, Terry 87–101
Perry, Brian 103–34, 129–30
Phillips, Barry 185
Pimpernel, The see Green, Mickey
Pinkas, Israel 140
Pointing the Finger see Midland Clearing
  Centre, Salford
police corruption 20, 259, 262
police perspectives 12
Potter, Lord Justice 159
Princess Margaret 66
Pritchard, Jack 41
Provisional IRA 197, 205–8

R
Ray, Maurice 43
Reynolds, Bruce (The Colonel) 27, 33–46
Richardsons 88
Riseley, Robin 104–6, 109
Rising Sun organization 181
Robinson, Brian 103–34, 114
Robinson, Tim 182
Rogers, Ken 48
Rowlands, Robert 57–65
Royle, Stuart 225, 228, 229
Rubin, Eric 137, 143
Rusha, Lea 219, 223–25

S
Sabin, Howard 47
Salford heist 151–60
Sampson, Melanie 214, 215
Saxe, Clifford 100
Scarface 142
Scotland Yard 21–2, 27, 41, 44–5, 62–5, 100, 111, 114, 115, 119, 120, 125, 161, 236
Scott, Gordon 129
Scouse, Michael 104–6, 108–10,
Seamarks, Pamela 137
Secricor 151–60, 259
Securitas Depot, Tonbridge (Tiger Attack) 209–31
Security Express depot, Shoreditch 87–101
Security Express van 69–86, 87
Segars, John (Chainsaw Gang member) 69–86
Serious Crimes Squad 22
Sewell, Jim 82
Shatford, Jon 166, 169, 171, 177–9
Sherlock Holmes 57
Sidhu, Harjit 190–2
Sidhu, Sundeep 185–7, 190, 192
Sinn Féin 206
Skoubon, Helle 144
Smalls, Bertie 22
Snow over Shoreditch see City of London
Spot, Jack 19, 53
Steiger, Martin QC 157
Stephens, Thomas 67
Steve (Baker Street bank robbery) 60–62
Stevens, Sir John 171
Stocker, Judge Justice 83
supergrasses 10, 22, 146
Sweeny, the 17, 18–

T
Taking the Mickey see Banstead, Surrey
Teramo, Italy (What Goes Around, Comes Around) 135–50
Thomas, Thomas 240, 244

Tiger Attack see Securitas Depot, Tonbridge
Tucker, Reginald 67

U
Unit 7 103–34

V
Vallorani, Agostino 140
Viccei, Valerio 135–50
Vlasov, Alexei 181
Volga, Operation 156, 160

W
walkie-talkie robbery 57–65
Walkie-Talkies Tell No Lies see Baker Street
Ward, Chris 197–208
Waring, Michael 174–5
Weak Spot see Heathrow Airport
Webb, Duncan 25
Welch, Robert (Bobby) 31–53
Wenham, Lee 179
What Goes Around, Comes Around see Teramo, Italy
Wheater, John Denby 31–53
Whitby, David 32, 33
White, Jimmy 45, 46
White, Joe 126
White, Tony 103–34, 116
Whitemore Prison escape attempt 121–2
White's Hotel, Bayswater 140
Who Played the Tune see Northern Bank, Belfast
Wickstead, Albert (the Grey Fox) 22
Wilson, Charles Frederick (Charlie) 31–53, 52
Windsor, Barbara 88, 98
Wisbey, Thomas William (Tommy) 31–53
Wolf, The see Viccei Valerio
Wolfe, Benjamin 67
Woolwich Crown Court 240, 242
Wright, Brian (Milkman) 133